The
Problem
with
Everything

The
Problem
with
Everything

My Journey Through
the New Culture Wars

Meghan Daum

Gallery Books

New York   London   Toronto   Sydney   New Delhi

G

Gallery Books
An Imprint of Simon & Schuster, Inc.
1230 Avenue of the Americas
New York, NY 10020

First Gallery Books hardcover edition October 2019

GALLERY BOOKS and colophon are
registered trademarks of Simon & Schuster, Inc.

For information about special discounts for bulk purchases,
please contact Simon & Schuster Special Sales at 1-866-506-1949
or business@simonandschuster.com.

The Simon & Schuster Speakers Bureau can bring authors
to your live event. For more information or to book an event,
contact the Simon & Schuster Speakers Bureau at 1-866-248-3049
or visit our website at www.simonspeakers.com.

Manufactured in the United States of America

1   3   5   7   9   10   8   6   4   2

Library of Congress Cataloging-in-Publication Data is available.

ISBN 978-1-9821-2933-0
ISBN 978-1-9821-2935-4 (ebook)

Dedicated to the memory of my father,
the original critical thinker

The half-truths, repeated, authenticated themselves.

—Joan Didion, "The Women's Movement," 1972

Contents

Introduction

This began as a book about feminism and only feminism. I started in the fall of 2016, on the cusp of what would obviously be Hillary Clinton's election to the presidency. The book was a critique of the current state of the women's movement. It wasn't going to make every feminist happy, but we were about to have a female president, so I figured they could handle it.

My criticisms were centered on what are sometimes referred to as the "excesses" of contemporary feminism. I was tired of what I saw as the movement's lack of shading and dimension. I was tired of the one-note outrage, the snarky memes, the exhibitionism, the ironic misandry in the vein of #KillAllMen, the commodification of the concept of "giving zero fucks" (the number of T-shirts for sale on Etsy displaying some iteration of DGAF, or "don't give a fuck," amounts to a genuine fuckton). I supported the fundamentals of the message, of course; women deserve equal status to men and should have autonomy over their bodies (at least these were the fundamentals as I saw them). But I was wary that the blustering tone of the media, social media especially, had set up an overcorrection that was veering into self-parody.

Feminism had achieved many of its goals, the passage of laws around equal pay and reproductive rights, the ability of wives to initiate divorce, and access to education for women, to name a few. There was more work to be done, of course. Which is why I was so worried that feminism was in danger, especially on the social media front, of becoming a noisepool—and from there an echo chamber—of manufactured or at least highly exaggerated problems. And these weren't problems as we usually think of them but, rather, everyday phenomena now reclassified as "problematic." Some of this problematica (my word) grew out of the sudden problematization (their word, alas) of masculinity. Men, with their unchecked power and privilege, were purveyors of intolerable scourges like mansplaining and manspreading. In fact, so unassailable was their power that women who bashed them could do no damage because these women were effectively "punching up" to unassailable male power. Articles like *Bustle*'s "6 Reasons Men Can Literally Never Be Victims of Sexism," *Jezebel*'s "Men (Wrongly) Think They're Smarter Than They Are" (that one dates back to 2008), and *Everyday Feminism*'s "160+ Examples of Male Privilege in All Areas of Life" were emblematic of that mentality—and endemic in the feminist blogosphere.

On its face, most of this stuff was too silly to get all

that exercised about. We know by now that a lot of what's on the internet is much ado about nothing. But what bothered me most about this new feminism was something more general—something ambient, really. What bothered me was the way the prototypical young feminist had adopted the sort of swaggering, wise-ass persona you see most often in people who deep down might not be all that swaggering or wise. This young feminist frequently referred to herself as a badass.

Originally, this book was going to be called *You Are Not a Badass*. Then Hillary Clinton lost the election to Donald Trump. Along the way, much of the country lost its appetite for the sort of critique I was offering. There is no doubt that had Clinton won, a special kind of pernicious and ugly sexism would have underscored her presidency. The badass feminists would still have had their hands full calling out all the sexist barbs—subtle and otherwise—aimed in Clinton's direction. But the way things turned out, there was no subtlety to be found. There was no room for left-on-left critique of any variety.

The word "tribal" was suddenly everywhere. It now referred not to ethnic ties dating back thousands of years but to more recently established affiliations of class and culture. According to the pundits, it was tribalism that had formed those information silos that kept us from seeing this coming. It was tribalism that had caused so many people to pull the lever for someone they found morally reprehensible yet somehow less threatening than the alternative. And though feminism occupied a large space in this expanding conversation about identity and American values, there was clearly now much more to talk about than silly memes and shallow expressions of badassedness (or, to use my preferred construction, badassery).

The country was falling apart. I now realize I was falling apart, too—at least a bit.

As with the country, my meltdown was already in progress by the fall of 2016, but up until then I'd been only partially aware of the extent of it. I knew I was experiencing some stress from (to borrow a term from insurance companies) a "qualifying life event," namely divorce. I knew I'd probably added to that stress by moving across the country by myself with no steady work and a Saint Bernard (the move was an effort to make a clean break from my marriage, since the marriage had never been quite bad enough to break cleanly on its own). What I did not fully comprehend were the ways in which my unrest ran deeper than divorce and relocation.

I was suddenly obsessed with aging—my own as well as that of others. I had up until then lived a life of precociousness, having mostly older friends and often being the youngest person in any given room. Now, though, my joints were literally and figuratively beginning to creak. I was hearing voices inside my head yelling the equivalent of "get off my lawn." I supported social justice causes as much as the next self-respecting liberal, yet I was irritated by the smug vibe of many young activists within the new left. This vibe was especially observable in the ones who had embraced the concept of being "woke," a term borrowed from the black civil rights movement that signaled one's allegiance to a more general ethos of progressive righteousness. (In the spirit of all of this, I coined my own term to describe the class of NPR-listening, *New Yorker*–reading, *Slate*-podcast-downloading elites once called the cognoscenti. They were now the wokescenti.)

Meanwhile, the pace at which the digital revolution was moving had me feeling old before my time, even physically dizzy on a near-daily basis. At my computer, the tweets and memes and hot takes scrolled down my screen so fast I could scarcely comprehend a fraction of them. Whereas my life had once felt like a road trip on which I was usually running ahead of schedule, I now felt like I was running on a treadmill, the mat churning beneath me at high speed while I held on to the handlebars for dear life. I wanted to slow the machine down so I could catch my breath. Sometimes I even thought it might be nice to go to sleep for five or ten years, until this madness somehow ran its course. The phrase "woke me when it's over" became a little in-joke with myself.

I hesitate to characterize this as a midlife crisis. That seems too generic in the same way it would be too generic to call the Trump election a political crisis (not that it wasn't; it was just so much more than that). As I think about it, I suspect the crisis I suffered was a personal one that happened to get intensified by the fallout of a political catastrophe.

That is not to say my personal problems were political or vice versa. I never much believed that the personal is political. As a slogan, "The personal is political" has a patina of earnestness, even gravitas, but, let's face it, more often than not the personal is just personal. In my case, the personal wasn't unique or even necessarily all that interesting.

Over time, I began to see the ways in which my wariness toward what I saw as hollow indignation and performed outrage—my resistance to certain aspects of the resistance, if you will—was in many ways fundamentally generational.

This book still has a lot to do with the conflicted and tortured state of liberalism generally and feminism in particular. But it's now also a personal story of feeling existentially unmoored against the backdrop of a country falling apart. It's a story about aging and feeling obsolete as the world spins madly—and maddeningly—on. It's also, by dint of my age, about the particular experience of Generation Xers, the last cohort to have experienced both the analog and the digital world as adults. Because of this—and for reasons I'll explain more later—we're also the first generation that younger generations don't especially want or need to look up to. Any wisdom we might have to share is already obsolete.

• • •

Introduction

If 2018 was the year that the concept of "cancel culture" went mainstream (foolish tweets caused Roseanne Barr to lose her show and Kevin Hart to lose his Oscars-hosting gig, the holiday song "Baby, It's Cold Outside" was shunned as an example of rape culture, the previously canceled Louis C.K. was secretly taped at a comedy gig and informed that he'd violated the terms of his banishment), then 2019 may be the year that cancel culture cancels itself. Late last winter, within just a few weeks of one another, two young-adult fiction authors withdrew their soon-to-be-published books when social media mobs attacked them for racial insensitivity. This was, for the most part, not based on anyone actually reading the books in question. Instead, it was the noxious effects of the approval vortex of "YA Twitter," a small but loud minority of readers who have perfected the art of ruining careers under the guise of social justice. One of these self-canceled authors was already known as a punishing patrolman of cultural appropriation and was even employed as a "sensitivity reader" for big publishing houses (this is a real job in which books are vetted for ways in which they may be offensive to marginalized groups). Needless to say, that detail made the whole affair an especially delicious example of the ways social justice activism was eating itself.

Around this same time, a devastating documentary about Michael Jackson's sexual abuse of children had people ·calling for his music to never, ever be listened to again. A few weeks before that, Jussie Smollett, a gay black television actor, had elicited torrents of sympathy and outraged solidarity when he reported being the victim of a crime where the perpetrators tied a noose around his neck and shouted "MAGA country!" After an investigation, police said they believed the actor staged the whole thing in an effort to gain publicity and, reportedly, boost his salary. Smollett denied these reports and maintained his innocence, and county prosecutors eventually made the controversial decision to drop all charges. The reasons behind this decision remain murky, but amid the official hand-wringing, this much seemed clear: two years into the Trump era, the weaponization of "social justice culture" was headed toward some kind of peak.

As for never again listening to Michael Jackson's music, all I can say is, seriously?

This is where we stand at the moment. Believe me, the shakiness of this ground terrifies me. I continue to be horrified and disgusted by the extreme anti-abortion measures proposed in states such as Alabama and Georgia in May. After being one of those skeptics who refused to believe *Roe v. Wade* would ever be overturned, I now think this fate is entirely possible (though I also fear the decision was based on a wobbly legal premise that, in some sense, was set up to eventually fail). So I get that these are bad times. Very, very, very bad times. But by framing Trumpism as a moral emergency that required an all-hands-on-deck, no-deviation-from-the-narrative approach to cultural and political thought, I fear the left has cleared the way for a kind of purity policing—enforced and amplified by social media—that is sure to backfire somehow or other. Even if we manage to get rid of Trump, either by voting him out of office in 2020 or somehow kicking him out before then, the political left still needs a course correction. We need to stop devouring our own and canceling ourselves. We need fewer sensitivity readers and more empathy as a matter of course. We need to recognize that to deny people their complications and contradictions is to deny them their humanity.

This book is a product of its times, which is in part to say it's a casualty of the news cycle that churns around it. Short of publishing this as a living document that I update around the clock to ward off the wolves of obsolescence (there's a *Black Mirror* episode in the making here), there is nothing I can do to keep this book from essentially being frozen in time as of the last proofreading pass. There have been moments in the months leading up to publication in which I've fretted that the focus on feminism, which felt so acute a few years ago, is now yesterday's baguette compared to fresher, more contemporary conversations about gender and race.

But the old adage "Write what you know" never becomes obsolete. A friend who will remain nameless put a new spin on that adage recently, advising me to "write about feminism, because as a straight, cisgendered, able-bodied, (mostly) heteronormative white chick, it's the only thing available to you anyway."

Much as I hate to duck out on my responsibility, I'm happy to use the current rules of authorship as an excuse for not writing more about other forms of identity-driven politics. Actually, let me rephrase that: I'm not necessarily happy to avoid it (I do have a few things to say). But I'm committed enough to saying what I have to say about basic, boring feminism and the generational divides therein to know better than to sabotage it by touching certain third rails of current public debate. (I'll let you guess as to what those third rails might be. As with so much in life, their potency is in the eye of the beholder.)

Some items of business before I wrap this up and get on with the show. I talk a great deal in the first half of the book about various waves of feminism. Definitionally, the first and second waves are pretty universally understood. The first wave refers to the nineteenth- and early twentieth-century movements around things like voting and property rights. The second wave refers to the 1960s and 1970s, the era of Gloria Steinem and *Ms.* magazine and collective action around reproductive rights and workplace equality.

After that, the terms get a little fuzzy. "Third wave," which was coined in the early 1990s by the writer Rebecca Walker (daughter of famous second-wave author Alice Walker, from whom she became estranged over their conflicting interpretations of feminism), I can really only describe as a mishmash of aesthetics that correspond with loosely defined philosophies: essentially rock bands with vague ideologies attached to them. From the riot grrrl scene to the sex-positive, reclaimed trashiness of the *Girls Gone Wild* franchise, the contradictions of the third wave were probably best captured by the feminist scholar Elizabeth Evans, who wrote that "the confusion surrounding what constitutes third-wave feminism is in some respects its defining feature."

This brings me to the fourth wave. When I say "contemporary feminism" in this book, I am talking primarily about the fourth wave. This is a feminism largely shaped by social media. If the imprimaturs of the second and third waves were the burning of bras and the wearing of Doc Martens boots, respectively (though, to be accurate, the bra burning happened far less frequently than is often assumed), the signature of the fourth wave is the hashtag, the eye-rolling GIF, and, more seriously, the beginnings of questioning the whole idea of a gender binary.

Fourth-wave feminism is heavily influenced by the theory of intersectionality, a framework for thinking about how different types of oppression and privilege can overlap and interact with each other. In a general sense, intersectionality can be a useful tool for understanding power structures, particularly economic ones, but, as I'll talk about, it's frequently reduced by fourth-wave feminism into a shorthand for wokeness, which itself is shorthand for an entire system of thought rooted in postmodernism and Marxism and a whole lot of other isms that most people don't think about when they're throwing the term around on Twitter. (Indeed, there is now a segment—or, more precisely, several intersecting segments—

of Twitter casually referred to as Woke Twitter. At its best, Woke Twitter elicits greater awareness and sensitivity around issues of social justice. At its worst, it functions as the purity police and calls people out for the slightest missteps beyond the bounds of intersectionalist doctrine.)

You may be wondering exactly what form this book purports to be taking. Is it a memoir? A manifesto? A report from the trenches of the culture wars? A series of essays? A series of arguments for which there is no winning, only crazy-making equivocation?

The answer is all of the above and none of the above. If I were forced to give it a label, I'd probably call the book an extended rumination, eight chapters of method-driven meandering. It consists of research and reporting as well as reflection and, at moments, occasionally inflamed, possibly unhinged gut reactions. Though I've changed the names of a few interview subjects to protect their privacy, most of the people who talked with me for this book did so on the record and transparently. Many of those conversations, like all great conversations, ended in a place we couldn't have anticipated when they started.

The same could be said for me in the writing of this book. The place I took off from three years ago is not the place where I've landed. And though I'm still not sure what to make of this terrain, I can tell you that the intellectual uncertainty into which it has forced me is a lot more interesting—and a lot more honest—than some of the convictions that carried me along before. If nothing else, this is a story of its time, which means it's a story for which we don't yet know the ending.

I've never been more afraid of writing a book. I've never been more certain I had to.

The
Problem
with
Everything

CHAPTER 1

....

Sign the Petition:
From the Meat Grinder to #MeToo

I remember a woman who screamed like a feral animal. She was leather tan and sinewy. Spiked bleached blonde hair, sculpted biceps, low-slung cargo pants with Doc Martens, veins bursting from her neck, eyes bugging from her drawn face. She stood on the sidewalks of New York City with a folding table covered with poster-size images from hard-core pornography: women wearing dog collars, women on leashes, women leaned over and viewed from behind, their backs crosshatched with scars. Much of the time she displayed a blowup of the famous *Hustler* magazine cover showing a naked woman being fed upside down into a meat grinder.

"This is what your husbands are masturbating to," she shouted in a barking monotone. "Wake up, women! Don't be passive! Sign the petition!"

Most everyone turned away or just kept walking. This was back in 1990. There were more people shouting things on the streets of New York City than there are now. Hare Krishnas ambled around Grand Central Terminal, Jews for Jesus yelled into megaphones in Times Square, and the obstreperously deranged were everywhere, mostly homeless, sometimes violent. The feral woman didn't have a homeless vibe to her—a squatting-in-an-East-Village-tenement-vibe maybe, but not a homeless one—but she was clearly a little berserk, if not deranged herself.

She could be spotted all over town, frequently in the East Village near Astor Place, but I passed her near Lincoln Center nearly every day during the summer of 1990. I was working as an intern—a paid one, $200 a week!—at the Film Society of Lincoln Center. I didn't know it at the time, but this was the best job I would ever have. I did little more than answer the phone, sort the mail, and test my adult conversational wings by trying to keep up with the endlessly witty banter in our open-space basement digs below Alice Tully Hall. At least one day a week, a male coworker with whom I'd become flirtatiously friendly would relieve me of my duties, such as they were, and take me to press screenings in luxurious Midtown screening rooms, after which we would go out for cheap Thai food. My first day on the job we saw the movie *Ghost* and agreed that it would be a total box office bomb.

I practically skipped to the office every morning. I was staying on the Upper West Side, apartment sitting in a sweltering fifth-floor walkup with an exposed-brick wall and a mouse problem. As with the perks of the internship, I did not at the time fully appreciate what a coup this arrangement was. I was twenty years old. Construction workers called out to me most mornings as I walked along Amsterdam Avenue and then over to Broadway. They did this not because I was inordinately eye-catching but (in yet another example of something I did not fully appreciate) because I was twenty years old. Depending on my mood, I ignored them, laughed at them, or gave them the finger over my shoulder, a gesture that felt like hailing a cab in reverse. The men were annoying, and sometimes the annoyance they caused registered as embarrassment and even shame. Mostly, though, they felt like homegrown nuisances, as integral to the New York experience as rats or corrupt landlords.

To be twenty years old in 1990 in New York City was, as far as I was concerned, to own the world. I owned practically nothing of material value back then, but somehow this was all part of a magical transaction in which I knew I'd eventually get ahead even if it seemed, for the moment, like I could barely keep up. The city was still a wild kingdom, a stone-and-steel fortress with rage burning inside. The crack epidemic was long under way and also a long way from ending. AIDS was everywhere—ravaging the bodies of the visibly ill, beckoning from public service announcements that preached condoms or death, scaring sexually active single people out of their minds. The graffiti was only beginning to come off the subway cars. The Tompkins Square Park riot was just two years gone by. The woman who'd become known as the Central

3

Park Jogger had been beaten, raped, and left for dead barely a year earlier. (And it would be more than a decade before the young men falsely convicted of the crime—convictions due in no small part to punitive grandstanding from local loud-mouth Donald Trump—would be exonerated.)

Every man, woman, and, yes, many children (including those commuting to fancy prep schools) had been mugged or knew someone who had. Every woman knew what it was like to be creepily rubbed against by some dude in a crowded space, and when this happened many of us either jammed our elbows into his abdomen or rolled our eyes and moved away. One time, as I walked down a mostly empty Columbus Avenue around midnight, a man walked up to me—a redheaded, bearded man perhaps ten years my senior—reached his hand out, and shoved me just below my left collarbone. It was a fairly hard shove, and I almost lifted my arm to shove him back. Instead, the moment passed and I just looked at him in disgust and confusion as we both continued along our way. I figured the guy was mentally ill or on drugs or both. I remember feeling grateful that the situation hadn't escalated into anything worse. (In retrospect, I realize how extraordinarily lucky I was, and how lucky I have been in other situations since.) What I don't remember is connecting the incident to anything like what would now be called institutionalized mi-sogyny. This was not systemic oppression of women. This was simply life in the big city.

Nearly thirty years later, the angry, ranting woman with the folding table is gone from the sidewalk. In her place are millions of angry women marching in the streets and, even more so, ranting online. We are tiny pixels coalescing into a giant portrait of rage in all its definitions. We are shouting at senators in elevators as they prepare to vote for the confirmation of Supreme Court justices accused of sexual assault. We are wearing the red robes and white bonnets of the dystopian *Handmaid's Tale* costume and protesting in front of statehouses where lawmakers are threatening reproductive rights. Celebrities are wearing #TimesUp pins on the red carpet. Women of every imaginable walk of life are joining the #MeToo chorus as if Handel had come back and written a new *Messiah* oratorio just for us. We are owning our anger, breathing fire rather than swallowing our rage. It's no longer just about signing petitions—it's about stopping the world as we've known it in its tracks.

What could you call the fall of 2017 other than the Fall of the Fall of Man? It was a season of hurricanes and rapid soil erosion, namely the mudslide that began with Harvey Weinstein and quickly pulled more men down with it than anyone could reasonably keep up with. Or maybe that's the wrong metaphor. Maybe it wasn't a mudslide as much as a giant oil spill from the tanker on which contemporary Western society had been carrying its assumptions about male behavior. Like fossil fuels themselves, this behavior had long been construed as a necessary evil, one for which any purported cure seemed as futile and flimsy as a reusable shopping bag. *(Hit him with your stiletto if he gets handsy! Make him get in touch with his feelings! Pry his eyes open and force him to read the SCUM Manifesto!)*

For the first time ever, though, a cure seemed possible. The pathogen had been isolated and identified. Research dollars were flowing. Trials were under way. Hope was in sight, if not for my generation then maybe for the next.

I'm not going to even try to summarize the events of that fall or list the men who went down in the spill of #MeToo. Entire books will be written about that movement, the best of which probably can't be embarked upon until enough years have passed to allow authors even a modicum of perspective. What I can tell you about the fall of 2017 is that it coincided with a downward slope of my youth that was far steeper than I had any grasp of at the time. The autumn of 2017 marked my second year back in New York City after being away for the better part of two decades, most of it in California. Though I'd left California in 2015 in the wake of irremediable, if mercifully amicable, marital separation, it had taken nearly two years to officially get divorced, and this new status carried a sting whose effects sometimes proved paralytic. How could I have imagined that replacing the license plates on your car could feel like a death? (Somehow I'd managed to keep my car registered in California until the last possible minute.) Who knew that shopping for a new health insurance policy could make you feel like you're on a plastic pool raft floating aimlessly in the Dead Sea? (Okay, I guess everyone knows that.)

I'd left New York when I was nearly thirty. I was now forty-seven. Whereas my chief experience of the city was that of a young woman, I was now faced with re-entering it as a middle-aged one. It wasn't just that I had been young in New York; New York *was* my youth. It was the place where I'd spent my entire twenties. It was the place where I figured out what kind of person I wanted to be. That's a different thing from actually figuring out how to be that person, and it took leaving New York to accomplish that task, but as they like to say in California, setting your intention is the most important phase of the journey. New York was the backdrop for my earliest triumphs and stupidities. It was the first and last place I ever lived where on any given night you could step outside and feel like absolutely anything could happen, that the course of your life could shift like a subway train switching from the local track to the express. It was the place where I had my first real job, my first grown-up boyfriend, my first martini, my first call from a debt collector, my first call from a hospital pay phone telling me someone was in serious trouble. It was the site of my earliest rough drafts and rough treatments, the ones visited upon me as well as the ones I inflicted on others.

Now that I had returned, it was as if my twenties were being handed back to me in used condition. What a strange remnant to hold in your hand. What a bittersweet walk down memory's plank. Here I was again, a girl alone and on the town. I was my most primordial self, a girl who was rabidly ambitious in some ways but inexplicably lazy in others. I was a girl who technically hadn't been a girl for the better part of thirty years but who nonetheless felt a strange remove from the word "woman," which seemed to convey a poise and seriousness I hadn't yet attained. I may have been in my mid-forties, but I was still all jokes and hammy self-deprecation, still unable to accept compliments, still flirting with men by defaulting to my best Diane Keaton in *Manhattan* impression, even though it had been decades since I was attracted to the kind of men who were attracted to that. I was all the things I'd been when I was young except for the young part. I had a nicer apartment, a little more money, and a little more professional recognition. I had a dog (this I'd longed for in my twenties the way some women long for babies) and a car that I had to move for alternate-side street cleaning. But my days were more or less the same. I sat at my desk and drank coffee. I did my work when I could, but more often I stared into space and wondered what would become of my life. I surfed the internet at a connection speed that would have been unimaginable in 1995.

In part because of that connection speed, the space I stared into most of the time wasn't my own physical space but some unholy rotation of social media, news media, and floating junk courtesy of cyberspace. By the time President Trump entered office, I probably spent at least three-quarters of my waking hours with my head in this space. By the time #MeToo reached full force, my brain no longer felt connected to my body. At times, my brain no longer felt associated with my brain as I'd once known it. There were moments in which I couldn't remember the names of people I'd been acquainted with for years. In intense, animated conversations with friends and colleagues, I'd find myself revving up to some sort of grand insight and then suddenly sputtering out mid-sentence, like a roller coaster propelled halfway up a loop but unable to make it all the way around. Bunched up in my desk chair, I would stare at the computer screen for hours, hunting for words as though tracking lions on safari and practically sweating from the exertion.

More than a few times I wondered if I was experiencing some form of dementia. One night I dreamt that a woman wearing a blazer and carrying a clipboard sat me down and informed me that based on a set of tests involving some obscure measurement (the length of my index finger? the distance between my hairline and the top of my ear?), it had been determined that I had very-early-onset Alzheimer's and would be senile well before my time. In the dream, I was devastated and terrified. Waking up, I was met with the same startled relief I'd felt back in my twenties when I'd awaken from dreams in which I was told I was pregnant or had tested positive for HIV.

These are phase-of-life dreams, of course, but they're also dreams of their particular eras of history. In the 1990s I dreamt of HIV, which was then a death sentence and which had loomed over my particular generational cohort as a runaway train that "didn't discriminate" and would plow into anyone, *anyone,* who dared to forgo a condom even one time. In the 2000s, in my thirties, I dreamt of real estate I longed for but couldn't afford. Now, in 2018, I was dreaming of dementia, and maybe for good reason. I once read that there's scientific proof of a correlation between increased nostalgia and creeping senility. And since returning to New York, I'd been soaking in nostalgia. Everywhere I went, my twenties played in my head like a song stuck there permanently. Every neighborhood, every subway station, in some areas every street corner, echoed with some memory from that time.

There was John's pizzeria on Bleecker, where, at twenty-one and playing hooky from college upstate, I sat with a man—a boy, really—who both was and wasn't my boyfriend and listened to him reminisce about his old girlfriend, who, he said, was "sexy without being pretty, if that makes any sense." There, at the corner of Eighty-Second and Broadway, was the Barnes & Noble where I remember searching for the bathroom while having a urinary-tract infection so painful it made my hands shake. There, among the slabs of buildings of midtown Sixth Avenue, were the offices of more temp jobs than I could count: banks, law firms, insurance companies, each with its own mini kitchen and passcode-protected employee restrooms. There, on Columbus Avenue, is where the redheaded man had shoved me hard as I passed. There, at Fifty-Seventh and Broadway is a Duane Reade pharmacy that was once Coliseum Books, a place where the feral woman had often stood and yelled "Sign the petition!" I remember being dumped on Delancey Street, kissed on Charles Street, having a strange and short-lived personal-assistant job in a musty apartment on Sutton Place.

I remember standing on the corner of Eighth Avenue and Forty-Ninth Street as hail rained down like shellfire one summer night following a long, somewhat drunken dinner with an older man in a powerful position whose meal invitations I dreaded but nonetheless felt obliged to accept. I remember pocketing the cab fare he'd given me and taking the subway home.

I remember a lot about that summer. I was twenty-five, in graduate school, and newly split up from a three-year relationship with a very good man who nonetheless made me feel like my life was wedged in a pair of pliers. I had recently undergone a significant shift in my writing—stumbling upon the personal essay after years of fussing with mediocre short stories—that would set the course of the next two decades of my career. I was staying out late at parties and at various gatherings but also staying up late at home, writing furiously. I was terrifyingly broke, with maxed-out credit cards and past-due student loan payments, though this destitution was unrelated to my allowing the aforementioned older man in a powerful position to buy me expensive meals. Those meals had started out as business lunches but then migrated into semi-business dinners. During these dinners, the man would tell me certain details about his personal life, which was in a state of acute crisis. Caller ID was not yet a household item, and I remember the sinking feeling I got every time I picked up the phone and heard his voice. Every once in a while, as a sort of gift to myself, I'd allow myself to turn him down. Most often, however, I accepted the invitations. I did so because there was in this transaction the implicit notion that he could help my career, albeit in a rather vague, abstract way. I did so because not accepting them felt like a kind of professional self-sabotage, as foolish and irresponsible as missing deadlines.

Things never got sexual with this man, though I got the feeling they almost certainly would have if I'd allowed them to. At one point he called me up and invited me to his country house for the weekend. I remember feeling sick to my stomach while issuing a perfunctory demurral about having too much schoolwork. He later wrote me a letter apologizing for that invitation, saying he hoped it didn't sound strange. At no time did he make an ultimatum or proposition me directly. Creeped out as I occasionally was, I never felt like I was being sexually harassed. Obviously no one was kidnapping me from my apartment and forcibly escorting me to the Oyster Bar, where the man would sit waiting for me, smoking probably the fourth of fifteen cigarettes he'd smoke that night.

I'll cop to a certain psychological gamesmanship on my part as well. I'd occasionally bum a cigarette from him, an act that gave me a sense of distance and control but that surely read to him as an intimate gesture. At least a few times, after I probably had one too many glasses of wine, I became rather suggestive and flirtatious, probing into his personal life, seeing how much I could get him to disclose as he got drunker and drunker. I did this in part as a defense mechanism. The more we talked about him, the less we talked about me. But I also did it because I wanted to mess with his head, and I was young enough then to think that doing so would serve as some kind of tacit punishment for his behavior. The truth, of course (which anyone but a young twerp would have the wisdom to realize), was that messing with his head was its own reward. I wasn't censuring his behavior as much as reinforcing it. As for my own, I've been cringing about it ever since.

Looking back, it would be easy to say I behaved like this out of some instinctive subordination to the man's power. There's an element of truth to that, but there's also an angle at which the situation could be viewed as quite the opposite. From this angle, I behaved the way I did because in some ways the power imbalance between the two of us was tipped in my favor. I was young and the man was twice my age. He may have had professional power over me, but it was limited and in no way unilateral. In fact, thanks to the personal details I'd siphoned out of him, I probably could have placed one phone call and made his life very difficult. And so I carried on with my coquettishness until somehow the meals became fewer and farther between and then finally ended, probably because he took up with someone else. I carried on this way because my life was an open horizon and his was an over-stuffed attic. I behaved this way because I must have known on some unconscious level that, at twenty-five, I had more of a certain kind of power than I was ever going to have in my life and that I might as well use it, even if the accompanying rush was laced with shame.

This was the summer of 1995. Alanis Morissette's *Jagged Little Pill* had come out that June, and I listened to it pretty much on constant repeat through August. One night, after doing my silly routine with this man and riding the subway home in self-disgust, I sat in my room and played *Jagged Little Pill* and then wandered into the kitchen to talk to my roommate. I remember grumbling to her about my dinner companion, complaining about his lechery while conveniently omitting the parts when I'd dramatically exhaled on my cigarette, looked him straight in the eye, and said something devastatingly witty and possibly a tiny bit dirty. (I'd like to add that I winked, but that wouldn't past the truth test, since I'm physically unable to wink.)

Instead I said, "God, what a perv."

"Sounds annoying," my roommate said. "But hey, you keep showing up. You must be getting something out of it."

During the Fall of the Fall of Man, I thought a lot about the showing up I'd done over the years. Every woman seemed to be taking this kind of inventory. It was like a novel everyone was reading, one with a plot that seemed easy enough to follow but whose underlying themes and messages amount to an abstruse thicket of personal projection and postmodern obfuscation. Like any sentient being, I'd been shocked and disgusted by the Weinstein revelations and saw no reason to equivocate about the reliability of his accusers or the severity of his punishment. But as the list of perpetrators piled up and the public censure piled on, the conversation around #MeToo (lacking a specific category, each new scandal was not a story or an issue but a "conversation") began to split down generational lines.

The first incident to put this divide in notably sharp relief involved a secret Google spreadsheet called the Shitty

Media Men list. This was an anonymously sourced, living document meant to warn women about certain men in the media business, mostly publishing, who were known for inappropriate sexual or sexually charged behavior. It included all kinds of men, from powerful editors and freelance writers, and described alleged misdeeds that ranged from "weird lunch dates" to inappropriate flirting to stalking to physical violence and all-out rape. And though the list was never officially published and disappeared from Google Docs almost as quickly as it emerged, enough screenshots were taken that the perpetrators became common knowledge almost immediately.

Within hours of the list's discovery, the chief line of inquiry around it, even more so than "Who started it?," was whether infractions like "weird lunches" should be lumped in with crimes like rape. Unsurprisingly, I found myself on the side of the oldsters who were deeply troubled not just by this "lumping" (again, there seemed to be only one operative word, and in this case it was "lump") but by the idea that anonymously sourced accusations could be made against publicly named people without warning or any sort of due process. "This is so wrong!" my same-age friends and I ranted. "You can't just do this! These millennials don't get it!" We said this as we forwarded the screenshots among each other, gawking at the names we recognized.

"Weird lunch!" I said to more than one person. "Welcome to publishing! I'm going to write a memoir about my early days in New York and call it *Weird Lunch*."

I laughed. And was legitimately appalled that the list, whether or not it had been meant to be kept secret, had been created in such a way that it could so easily go public. (Weren't millennials supposed to understand the viral forces of technology better than anyone?) But I also found myself looking back uneasily at my own weird lunches, especially the ones that had turned into weird dinners at the Oyster Bar. Those dinners, in turn, had caused me to act weird, and that memory of weirdness was cringeworthy enough to cause me to cancel out most of my memories of my dealings with the guy. I honestly hadn't thought of him more than a handful of times in nearly two decades. In fact, so far back in my mind had I shoved these memories that, days after the Shitty Media Men story erupted, I managed to read a #MeToo-related Facebook post describing someone who sounded uncannily like this man and yet brush it off as a coincidence.

I almost marvel at the level of my denial. The post referred to creepy lunches with innocent young aspiring female writers. It talked about women going out of their way to avoid him. Someone used the term quid pro quo. I skimmed the post and thought to myself that even though the man in question sounded like my old dining companion he almost certainly was not. After all, this post was about feeling victimized, which was not a word I'd ever applied to my situation.

A solid week passed before I allowed myself to admit that it was the same guy. In fact, I felt less and less inclined to know. Maybe because knowing would have forced me to place myself among those who didn't avoid him—at least not as often as I could or should have. That in turn would have forced me to ask myself if I'd had—and perhaps still had—a higher threshold for male nonsense than some other women. If the answer to that question was yes, was that a sign of strength or obtuseness? If the answer was no, would I be forced to admit that on some level I was consciously manipulating this man for the sake of my career? (Never mind that his ability to do anything for my career was negligible at best; "quid pro quo" was not how I would have described things.) I didn't like either of these interpretations.

More than that, though, I didn't like being reminded that twenty years had passed since those weird lunch days. And as the "conversation" lurched along and the narrative of the "generational divide" became the default narrative, I found myself reminded of this passage of time on a daily, even hourly, basis. When a scandal broke involving the actor and comedian Aziz Ansari, I felt that my membership on Team Older Feminist was so official that I might as well take out a charge card at Eileen Fisher and call it a day (though has anyone under forty ever used a "charge card"?). That scandal, in case you're lucky enough to have forgotten the details, involved an anonymous twenty-three-year-old woman telling a twenty-two-year-old web reporter named Katie Way the story of a very bad date with Ansari. The woman, who called herself "Grace," accused Ansari of failing to pick up on her "verbal and non-verbal cues" during a sexual encounter. Though she was not physically barred from walking out and never said no outright, Grace nonetheless felt violated by the encounter, calling it "by far the worst experience with a man I've ever had." (Ansari, for his part, said he perceived it as entirely consensual.) The date had taken place months earlier. It was only when Grace saw Ansari on television wearing a #TimesUp pin at the Golden Globe Awards in January of 2018 that she decided to come forward.

If the Shitty Media Men story had caused many of the older crowd to murmur quietly about whether things had gone too far, the Ansari story elicited a collective "Oh, no you don't!" It wasn't just the sloppy randomness of the whole presentation—the woman's testimony appeared as a poorly rewritten "as told to" on a little-known website and included an especially self-defeating detail about Ansari not serving his date her preferred type of wine—but the way it threatened to upset the very apple cart that had carried it in. You could just hear the thirty-five-and-older crowd shouting at their laptops, *Stop right there! This is not what we mean!* Watching the saga unfurl, I was reminded of the way Hillary Clinton supporters reacted during the 2008 election when, days after she had lost the Democratic presidential nomination, Sarah Palin appeared out of nowhere and started making noises about being a feminist and breaking the glass ceiling. *That's not what we meant! It doesn't work like this!*

And so the ground began to shake around the fault line. The older feminists scolded the younger ones for not being tough enough to take care of themselves. *If the construction worker whistles at you, give him the finger! If the drunk guy sitting next to you at the wedding reception gets fresh, kick him in the shins!* In turn, the youngsters chastised the oldsters for enabling the oppressive status quo with cool-girl posturing. *We shouldn't have to suppress our humanity by letting insults roll off us! We shouldn't have to risk our safety with physical violence because patriarchal norms have taught the drunk wedding guest he can act like that!*

Neither side was entirely wrong, of course. But both sides were talking past each other in ways that suggested there was no meeting in the middle. In the *New York Times,* Daphne Merkin identified a gulf between what women said publicly about #MeToo and the eye-rolling that went on in private. "Publicly, they say the right things, expressing approval and joining in the chorus of voices that applaud the takedown of maleficent characters who prey on vulnerable women in the workplace," she wrote. "In private it's a different story. 'Grow up, this is real life,' I hear these same feminist friends say."

In the *Atlantic,* Caitlin Flanagan, whose tendency toward a certain impish prudery has never made her popular among young feminists, wrote that the Ansari fracas, at least the version of it chronicled on Babe.net, constituted "3,000 words of revenge porn." She decried the helplessness of "a whole country full of young women who don't know how to call a cab."

On cable news, HLN anchor Ashleigh Banfield looked straight into the camera and addressed "Grace" directly.

"What you have done in my opinion is appalling," said Banfield, calling the allegations "reckless and hollow" and charging Grace with having "chiseled away at a movement that I along with all of my sisters in the workplace have been dreaming of for decades."

This being cable news, Banfield's producers invited Katie Way to appear on the show. And this being the digital era, Way declined the offer not with a "no thanks" but by popping off an e-mail that called Banfield a "burgundy lipstick bad highlights second wave feminist has-been" and noted that "no woman my age would ever watch your network."

Banfield shot back by reading parts of the e-mail on the air. Then she addressed Way directly.

"If you truly believe in feminism," Banfield said, "the last thing you should do is attack someone in an ad hominem way for her age. . . . That's not the way we have those conversations as women or as men. We don't attack—as journalists—we do not attack people for their age, or their highlights, or their lipstick. It is the most hypocritical thing a woman who says she supports the women's movement could ever do."

From there, it was game on, gloves off. It was young versus old. Eileen Fisher versus ironic high-waisted mom jeans. Aging women with burgundy lipstick and blonde highlights versus young women with tattoos and hair rebelliously streaked with blue dye. At least that was the prevailing narrative. There was a handful of generational dissenters. Bari Weiss, a then thirty-four-year-old writer and editor on the *New York Times* opinion page (who had edited the Merkin article, incidentally), came out swinging against Grace, saying the only thing Ansari was guilty of was not being a mind reader. My Facebook feed also turned up the requisite smattering of middle-aged women offering stories of long-ago icky dates they'd suddenly been given permission to reinterpret as injurious. But by and large, the generational-divide idea, while too simplistic, remained the easiest idea to work with. It was the one I kept returning to when I thought back on my twenties and the various emotional and even potentially physical injuries that I had chalked up to life in the big city. It was the one that elicited the mightiest swells of self-righteousness (*why can't they be tough like we were?*) alongside the cruelest glimpses of my mortality or, worse, my expendability (*they don't really care what we think at all, do they?*).

The week of the Ansari dustup was an unsettling week for me in an unsettling season. I was about to turn forty-eight. Though I'd been glued to the #MeToo commentary for months and was duly transfixed by the Ansari story, I hadn't been able to bring myself to enter the public fray. I had an intuitive sense of my general positions and opinions, but I was having trouble attaching them to words that seemed halfway original or interesting. It was worse than that, even. I felt confused a lot of the time, dazed by the speed at which the world was moving, simultaneously befuddled by and bored with the digital universe. I felt an ambient intellectual exhaustion pretty much constantly. I woke up feeling hungover even if I'd had no alcohol for days. I felt dizzy while sitting perfectly still. I was often certain that it was one p.m. even if it was six p.m. I felt blindsided by time itself.

The week of the Ansari dustup was the same week that Dolores O'Riordan, lead singer of the 1990s Irish rock band the

Cranberries and all-around Gen X style hero, died at forty-six. It was the same week that Elizabeth Wurtzel, a writer who was both the femme fatale and the bête noire of the 1990s literary scene, announced that, at forty-eight, she had advanced breast cancer. I knew neither of these women personally, but their news shocked me nearly to tears. That same week, some long-avoided internet research forced me to resign myself to the likelihood that I was in perimenopause, a sort of prodrome menopause that can last years and can, within the span of an hour, induce enough rage to topple over a refrigerator followed by enough horniness to have sex with whatever's in front of you, including that same refrigerator. It can also make you dizzy, headachy, and unable to think of the right words for things.

How devastatingly obvious it all was. My distress and confusion were as much hormonal as they were political, cultural, or personally situational. I didn't have dementia, but the dream about having Alzheimer's had obviously been a communication from my subconscious, a courtesy call from the future. In lieu of writing, I spent my days trying to beat back migraines, fantasizing about sex with strangers while exhaustively reading comments on Talking Points Memo. I scrolled through social media posts as if digging through sand for a lost item, lingering for hours on those that reinforced my view and dwelling for days upon those that inflamed me.

Once upon a time, I would have channeled my rage and lust into deep thoughts and big plans. I would have sat in my room listening to Alanis Morissette while jotting down notes for my next opus. I would have gone out onto the street and walked past the feral woman yelling "Sign the petition!" and caught a contact high from all of her fury and insanity. Riding those fumes, I might have taken myself to a movie or called a friend from a pay phone to say, "Hey, I'm in your neighborhood." Better yet, I might have gone home and written for eight hours with an urgency and focus that now seems as distant a memory as my youth itself. Today, I spend much of that time gawking at "sick burns" in Twitter arguments, trying to pinpoint the moment when people became so much crueler than they used to be, and also so much more fragile.

As I watch the world whiz past me on my computer screen, sharpened by the reading glasses I've lately been forced to wear while also dulled by decades of learning how to care a little less about things that are painful to care about, I wonder if my real problem with young feminists—with young activists in general—is that many of them are insufficiently awed by toughness. They didn't boast about it as children. They don't value it inordinately as adults. They refuse to be shamed by vulnerability. In fact, in a brilliant move of jujitsu, many have figured out how to use their thin skin as their most powerful weapon. My particular brand of toughness, it turns out, no longer holds much currency.

Maybe what we saw as sassy intrepidness just looked to younger women like wrinkles or age spots. Amid the #MeToo tweetstorm, I'd feel a particular pang when I saw the young feminists dismiss the older ones by pure virtue of their age. Never mind the substance of Flanagan's arguments, it was her pearls and sweater sets that rendered her not worth listening to. Merkin's op-ed, someone said, might as well have been titled "Boomer Uncomfortable with Change." This was a more generous comment than those that asked, simply, "Who the hell is Daphne Merkin?"

Merkin, an established critic and essayist, is about fifteen years older than I am. A year or so later, she would send the Twitter feminists into yet further spasms by publishing a *New York* magazine profile of Soon-Yi Previn that cast doubt on Mia Farrow's charges that Woody Allen had molested his daughter Dylan. She would disclose in the article that she was a longtime friend of Allen's, and that alone was enough to get her written off once and for all. Never mind that when *New York Times* columnist Nicholas Kristof disclosed that he was a longtime friend of Farrow's and devoted his column to Dylan's side of the story, he was lauded as a champion of women.

My opinions on the Allen-Farrow affair notwithstanding, it made me sad to see young women, especially young women journalists, dismiss a writer they might be able to learn from. I've never met Merkin, but given her age relative to mine she was right in the sweet spot of the kind of writer I looked up to when I was very young. At twenty-five, I not only wanted to know people like Daphne Merkin, I wanted to *be* them. There were hundreds of writers and artists in my imaginative orbit—some of them over fifty or possibly even sixty—whom I felt this way about. I knew none of them, but I wanted to be all of them. Together, they formed a great phalanx of wise elders whose only duty to me was to be themselves. My duty, in turn, was to watch and learn. By which I mean that was my duty to myself.

But something was different back then. I shared a planet with those elders. We occupied the same universe. We breathed the same air. I had the great gift of being able to look up to my elders because it was possible to be like them. We may have been of different generations, with different problems and preoccupations and ideas about what constituted paying a lot of rent, but we still all grew up holding books in our hands. We called our friends from pay phones and negotiated sexual situations without technological assistance and registered opinions without being smacked down on social media moments later. We made mistakes in private and, in turn, respected the privacy of others in their mistakes.

The same cannot be said for the relationship between my generation and those that are coming up behind us. Young people don't want to be us because they're not even the same species as us. Even if they did want to be us, the proposition would be absurd, like a human trying to emulate an orangutan. The world has changed so much between my time and theirs that someone just ten years younger might as well belong to a different geological epoch. In this epoch, there are no pay phones for calling friends at the spur of the moment. The contact highs from walking down the street have been replaced by dopamine hits from Instagram likes. To a young person, someone like me is not so much an elder as an extinction. Is it any wonder, then, that older generations' contributions to the conversation are, at best, a kind of verbal meteor shower, the flickering, nattering remains of planets that haven't existed for eons?

So this is where I find myself. In my dizziness and confusion, in my exhaustion and exasperation and pathetic, aphasic lust, I have wandered into a devastating but oddly beautiful revelation: my generation will be the last to have known the world in its analog form. As a result, we've grown old before actually getting old. We've become dinosaurs before we're even fifty. We've felt the pace of evolution shift suddenly into hyper-speed, leaving us lumbering along like primitive creatures as these sleeker humans glide past us.

And it's here, from this primitive-creature vantage point, that I find myself pressed up against yet another revelation: the questions we face now when it comes to men and women are questions that arose a split second ago. Modern humans have been around for some two hundred thousand years. Civilization as we know it has been churning away for perhaps six thousand years. Until the birth control pill came along in 1960, we were all essentially prisoners of nature, with women's conditions being markedly worse, sometimes obscenely so. Until 1960, the idea that women could compete with men in the job market, that men should do housework, that women had any purpose in life higher than having babies and men had any purpose higher than financially supporting those babies or going to war to protect them, was something close to unthinkable. That we have come so far in so little time is a marvel. That we should expect all the kinks to have been worked out by now is insane.

In the scheme of things, the fifty-nine years that have elapsed between 1960 and today is a nanosecond, a flash of time so imperceptible that it has passed in increments of billions by the time you have read this sentence. It was already nearly thirty years ago that the feral woman was out there with her folding table yelling "Sign the petition." It was already nearly thirty years ago that, as far as I was concerned, I owned the world. It feels like yesterday. Then again, every day feels like yesterday. Every day becomes yesterday before you know it.

CHAPTER 2

....

Growing Up Zooming:
A 1970s Childhood

I was not a good girl. By which I mean I was not good at being a girl. I hated dolls. I hated playing dress up. I had no interest in toy baby carriages or toy ovens or carrying around a little purse. I wasn't all that keen on most other girls, especially the primping, preening kind who were always in some state of hair brushing or lip glossing. Part of this had to do with my innate temperament, which has always erred on the side of a certain tomboyishness. Part of it had to do with my mother's innate temperament, which I could never really put my finger on but which she projected onto me as though I were not only her daughter but also her personal side mirror. My mother adamantly did not want me to be a "girly girl." This was a term she used frequently and whose reach included just about any of my female peers who giggled, wore nail polish, or carried purses in elementary school. She seemed, in fact, *afraid* of my being a girly girl, so much so that she never once dressed me in pink, put a bow in my hair, or pointed anywhere near the direction of makeup.

My mother was born in 1942. This timing made her a member of that unenviable cohort of women for whom second-wave feminism had come just slightly too late to make full use of. By the time women were shouting about equal division of housework, my mother had two kids and a husband, who, though hardly in the Don Draper mold, would never have given a passing thought to cooking a meal or mopping the floor. Though she aligned herself with the women's movement as fervently as any of her liberal friends in her quasi-academic circles (one of my favorite photographs shows my mother and a friend standing in front of a Planned Parenthood clinic in Terre Haute, Indiana, in 1969), feminism for her was something that was grafted onto her identity as a wife and mother.

For her, at least in those years, being a feminist meant raising a daughter in accordance with the feminist standards of the moment. It meant buying Marlo Thomas's *Free to Be . . . You and Me* record and singing along with celebrities like Alan Alda and Rosey Grier on songs about how boys can have dolls and how it's all right to cry. It meant making fruitless attempts to teach your children to say "firefighter" instead of "fireman." It meant pointing out chauvinism when the occasion called for it—"That man at the car repair shop was a chauvinist!"—and eschewing displays of chivalry: one afternoon at a swimming pool when I was about eight, I was so bewildered when a young boy gestured for me to jump off the diving board before taking his turn that I skulked away in confusion and shame. It was one of those childhood moments that by all rights should be utterly forgettable, yet for some reason has never left the surface of my memory. For nearly forty years, the moment has floated there like algae, which is apt because it took place at a rather dank indoor pool contaminated with who knows what. This was probably around 1978, at a Holiday Inn in some southern or midwestern town off the interstate. No doubt my family was making the drive to see relatives in Southern Illinois, and no doubt the peak experience of the trip for me was getting the chance to swim in a motel pool.

As a kid, I loved pools of all kinds but took a particular delight in motel pools, especially the indoor ones, where the colliding odors of chlorine and mold must have set off some kind of dopamine explosion in my brain. Just walking into those places, towel in hand, Mickey Mouse flip-flops on my feet, caused me to nearly combust from excitement. I can still remember the architecture of the pool complex at this particular Holiday Inn—"the Holidome," it was called. I remember the vaulted ceilings, the fluorescent lights, the grimy green tint of everything. I remember approaching the diving board and waiting while a boy around my age began to mount the short ladder.

Though he was clearly ahead of me in line, the boy stepped back when he saw me and motioned for me to go first. The way I remember it, he had a military-style haircut and his military-looking parents sat in nearby lounge chairs. At the other end of the pool sat my mother in her own lounge chair, probably tending to my younger brother with one hand while trying to balance a Judith Guest novel in the other. Catching her eye, I could see that she could see what was happening, though her reaction was such a jumble of signals that I had no idea what to make of them. She appeared to be shaking her head and nodding it at the same time. *Go. Don't go. Say thank you. Say no thank you.* Finally, I just walked away, avoiding eye contact with the boy as I shuffled alongside the pool back to my mother. The look on her face registered both disappointment and exasperation, though with whom I wasn't sure.

"That's something boys are taught to do with girls sometimes," she explained. "They're taught to let girls go first. He was being polite, but it's a form of chauvinism."

Mortified, I insisted that we leave the pool immediately. Which is really saying something, considering how totally awesome that Holidome was and how amazing the chlorine and mold smelled.

I was born in 1970. For the first few years of my life I was dressed almost entirely in yellow, which was also the color scheme of my nursery, such as it was (it was in fact a closet in my parents' student-housing apartment). My mother's opposition to the gender-coded colors of pink and blue meant she had to search hard to find alternative colors, and somehow yellow was the one that was most available. Thirty years later, when my friends were having babies, I would attend showers that were practically tributes to either pink or blue. Everyone found out their baby's sex ahead of time, which gave them months to conjure a fantasy version of their child based solely on that information. It wasn't until the late 1980s that it became common to learn the sex of your child before birth, and I wonder sometimes if the advent of this development didn't play some sort of subtle role in the almost cartoonish manifestations of gender we saw in the late nineties through the mid-aughts. Are newborn baby girls who come home to nurseries tricked out in lace and taffeta naturally set up for toddlerhoods of tiaras and fairy wings? Do those fairy wings later carry those girls to the sands of spring break in Cancún, where they strut about in thong bikinis and flash their breasts into live cams? In other words, is fetal ultrasound technology responsible for the hyper-aestheticization of the gender binary? (Paging all sociology and gender-theory scholars in search of research-paper topics: You're welcome!)

In any case, here's the thing about being raised in the 1970s. A more androgynous time has probably never existed in modern American history. In the 1975 Sears catalog (the Amazon.com of its time) less than 2 percent of toys were marketed specifically to boys or girls. Television ads showed children of both sexes playing with a range of toys in colors like green and yellow. The PBS kids show *Zoom*, which came out of WGBH in Boston and aired originally from 1972 to 1978, was a pageant of gender neutrality. Its cast of seven kids wore identical shirts, most memorably the blue-and-maroon-striped rugby shirts of the early years. They performed skits that had to do with jokes or made-up languages or science experiments. *Zoom*'s conceit was that young viewers were supposed to write in and suggest ideas for the show. Each week, the *Zoom* kids sang a little rap song that gave out the mailing address, and the song became such an earworm that I suspect a good portion of Generation X knows that Boston zip code—02134—as readily as we know the pledge of allegiance.

When *Zoom* was revived in 1999, it's worth noting that the rugby shirts were traded for more colorful fare and occasionally a girl or two could be spotted in pink. The show still had the same DIY bent, but it felt slicker, more focus-grouped. The hallmark of the show in both incarnations was the opening sequence, a choreographed song-and-dance number in which the kids introduced themselves one by one. "I'm Shona!," "I'm John!" they'd shout while momentarily displaying some talent or interest that the show's producers had decided to highlight. These talents involved a lot of running and tumbling and musical-instrument playing. Racial diversity was clearly a priority from the beginning; black, Asian, and Latino kids are all duly represented alongside the white kids. But to watch the 1970s sequences is to notice something subtle yet unmistakable about the cast: they are not boys and girls. They are kids. Obviously you can tell the boys from the girls, but as a collective they seem stripped of gender. There's a pure, unburnished quality to them that seems as raw and muted as the film stock.

Granted, it might in fact *be* the grainy, muted 1970s film stock that's creating this effect. But if you watch the opening sequence of a 1970s *Zoom* and compare it with the one from nearly thirty years later, you see more than a historical time-line of set design and special effects. You see girlness morph into girliness. You see magic wands replaced with pompoms. You see Carolyn with her tennis racket in 1976 (the idea being *she loves tennis!*) become Rachel with her hats and spar-kly crown in 2001. You see Shona with her toy piano in 1976 become Kaleigh with a magically appearing rack of T-shirts (*she's a clotheshorse!*) in 2001.

In fairness, these are some of the most glaring examples. The *Zoom* brand being what it is (or was), it's not like the new version was ever going to look like a Disney movie. More-over, while the *Zoom* aesthetic may have epitomized 1970s androgyny, there was still plenty of hyper-sexualizing of women going on in other corners of the culture. There was the Farrah Fawcett poster and *Charlie's Angels* and a cultural obsession with the Dallas Cowboys cheerleaders. There was the birth of the porn industry. On another bandwidth en-tirely, Phyllis Schlafly was fighting the ERA on the grounds that women are essentially a protected class and shouldn't give up a good thing.

You almost have to hand it to Schlafly. She went around decrying feminism by being the most in-your-face unapolo-getic power broad we'd seen since Ayn Rand. She had six kids and hated the Equal Rights Amendment, yet had a law de-gree and an enormous career that was about as "lean in" as it gets. If she wasn't some kind of twisted, primordial specimen of ideological contradiction, then I don't know who is. That was the thing about the 1970s; for every Farrah Fawcett poster, it seemed there was a no-nonsense woman leading by austere and sincere example. In 1972, Shirley Chisholm, the first black woman ever elected to Congress, ran for president. In 1973, ninety million television viewers tuned in to watch Billie Jean King beat card-carrying chauvinist Bobby Riggs in the historic "Battle of the Sexes" tennis match. In 1981, King left her husband and became the first mainstream public figure to come out as a lesbian (though the reveal was largely because her longtime girlfriend had come forward and sued her for money earned over the seven years of their relationship). The press, of course, feigned shock, but in reality it was hardly surprising. King had always looked like a lesbian. That is to say, she looked like a certain kind of woman of the 1970s.

I was only three years old in 1973, but I was already old enough to internalize certain aesthetic signifiers and unconsciously categorize them as aspirational versus non-aspirational. Aviator glasses, such as those worn by Billie Jean King and Gloria Steinem, were aspirational (I imagined my future self wearing these). Rugby shirts like those worn by the kids on *Zoom* were aspirational (not to mention easily attainable in the here and now). Phyllis Schlafly and Farrah Fawcett were non-aspirational figures, albeit it in totally different ways. My idols were serious types like Nadia Comaneci and Jodie Foster. I downright worshipped Jodie. I saw her Disney movies like *Freaky Friday* and *Candleshoe*. When the original

Freaky Friday came out in 1976, I begged to see it over and over again. I longed to be Jodie's character, Annabel Andrews. I wanted to wear a red-and-white-striped boatneck sweater (what was it with the seventies and stripes?) and play field hockey the way she did.

What does it say that the biggest child movie star of the 1970s, Jodie Foster, later came out as a lesbian? What does it say that one of the biggest child television stars, Kristy McNichol, was, too? Those actresses mapped proto-queerness over every Disney film and ABC drama they appeared in. Except it didn't read as androgyny at the time. As with the kids on *Zoom,* it read like standard kidhood. In the gender-neutral zone of this kidhood, girls didn't watch Disney princess movies. We watched *The Bad News Bears* right alongside the boys. We were allowed to identify with our personhood before our girlhood or boyhood. I believe this is one of the great gifts of being a member of Generation X. I also believe it's a big part of the reason many feminists my age have a hard time relating to younger feminists. We got to be girls on our own terms. We got to be kids, not just girls.

In 1975, I sat on the steps of the Texas Capitol with my mother, rallying with thousands of others on behalf of the passage of the Equal Rights Amendment. Women in bell-bottom pants and bandanna head scarves carried signs reading "Safe Legal Abortions for All Women" and "My Body My Choice." Surely a few of them wore the T-shirt, made famous by Gloria Steinem, that read "This Is What a Feminist Looks Like." I was five years old, wearing a smock-like peasant blouse over pants. I know this was my outfit because a woman sitting nearby with a sketchpad made a charcoal drawing of me that day. For as long as I can remember, that drawing, which my mother mounted behind frameless glass, was hung on the wall of her bedroom. The ERA never passed, of course. It was ratified by thirty-five of the thirty-eight states needed in order for it to become a constitutional amendment and even supported by President Nixon. But after nearly a decade of bouncing around various legislative houses, it never got there. Seven years later, the lack of ratifications led the Supreme Court to effectively kill the amendment by declaring it moot.

I remember hearing the news on National Public Radio while sitting in the kitchen doing homework as my mother cooked dinner. I remember asking who would be opposed to something as obvious as equal rights for women, and I remember my mother saying something about Phyllis Schlafly.

"But why would a woman be against equal rights for women?" I asked.

"I have no idea," my mother said.

It was 1982. I'd spent my early childhood in Austin, Texas, surrounded by hippies and academics, but we now lived in a Republican-leaning New Jersey suburb, one whose bland affluence would become blander and more affluent as the Reagan years trotted along. Just about every woman who lived in that town was a mom, and I think it's fair to say that very few worked full-time outside of the home. Still, 1982 was the year the phrase "having it all" entered the public lexicon. That was the title of Helen Gurley Brown's best-selling guide to all-around female fulfillment. And even though her advice ran along the lines of sleeping with your boss and subsisting on diet Jell-O in order to stay thin, "having it all" would serve as the operative catchphrase for white middle-class female ambition for the next decade at least.

By now we had entered the era of the Jane Fonda workout, the "coffee achiever" ad campaign (in which luminaries ranging from David Bowie to Kurt Vonnegut to Cicely Tyson were enlisted by the National Coffee Association to make coffee seem cool to young people), and, of course, "power dressing" for women. The last one, a sartorial project that sought to lend masculine traits to the female presentation in the workplace, was responsible for some of the worst looks in fashion history. (As for the former, go to YouTube, search for "coffee achiever," and be prepared to gasp at how long ago the 1980s look to be, not to mention the strangeness of Kurt Vonnegut appearing in a television ad.)

The number of women in the workplace had been rising steadily for the past several decades. Moreover, women in poor and working-class sectors had always done paid work outside the home. But the media was newly obsessed with the image of women commuting to high-rise office buildings every day, briefcases in hand and stiletto pumps on feet. (The impracticality of getting to work in high heels led to the trend of pairing running shoes with business suits for commuting purposes and changing into heels at the office.) The weekly newsmagazines churned out a steady rotation of stories about women with huge hair and huge shoulder pads making huge strides for all of womankind. I was only twelve, but these images danced inside my imagination like flashes from my future. I couldn't wait to grow up and wear a power suit with Nikes and carry my high-heeled shoes in my briefcase.

I suspect my mother wanted to put on some version of a power suit, too. The ERA might not have passed, but surely her children were old enough and the culture (even the culture of our stultifying Reaganite town) had changed enough for her to leave the house every morning without feeling like she'd committed an act of criminal negligence. It was the 1980s, after all. The next year, in 1983, Sally Ride would join the crew of the space shuttle *Challenger* and become the first woman in space. The year after that, Geraldine Ferraro would run for vice president and be the first woman nominee on a major-party ticket in a presidential race. Women were doing and having it all. What could possibly stop her from doing and having the same?

Plenty, as it turned out. This was the 1980s. Suddenly, it seemed that the job of motherhood included acting as a round-the-clock security detail. This would be difficult to combine with having an actual job.

"Concerning the cultural legacy of Etan's disappearance, we have created millions of helicopter parents who have spawned a generation or so of emotionally stunted children due to this extremely rare tragedy."

These words were written to me in an e-mail from Stan Patz, father of Etan Patz, a six-year-old boy who vanished from the streets of SoHo in 1979. Etan's disappearance set off a nationwide panic that changed the nature of parenting—and, moreover, childhood—forever.

I had a brief correspondence with Stan Patz in 2015. The case was back in the news because a man named Pedro Hernandez, who'd been eliminated as a suspect decades earlier, was on trial for killing Etan based on new evidence. I wrote a newspaper column about the case, specifically its role in the phenomenon that would eventually become known as helicopter parenting. I mentioned in the column that I thought there was insufficient evidence against Hernandez. Patz disagreed with me on that (and, indeed, the jury had found Hernandez guilty), but we exchanged a few cordial e-mails, one of which included his startling remark about the legacy of Etan's disappearance. I never forgot it.

By the 1980s, two high-profile child abductions, those of Etan Patz in 1979 and Adam Walsh in 1981, kicked off a massive movement around a supposed epidemic of missing children. (A horrific string of murdered children and teenagers in Atlanta added further to the sense of panic.) Photos of the missing children, along with their vital statistics and details about when and where they were last seen, appeared on billboards, pizza boxes, grocery bags, and, most famously, milk cartons. The effect was nothing less than macabre. These images wallpapered the public consciousness and suddenly turned childhood itself into a form of personal endangerment. The media, always hungry for a story too sensational to check, happily ran with the "epidemic" narrative, repeating the widely disseminated statistic that a million and a half children were reported missing each year.

Though there was no denying the horror of the Atlanta murders, the epidemic of vanishing children was never even close to being true. The faces on the pizza boxes and milk cartons were overwhelmingly those of runaways or kids who'd been taken by non-custodial parents during divorce and custody battles. Incidents of vanished children who had been taken by strangers were, so to speak, vanishingly rare. In 1984, the FBI investigated just sixty-seven cases involving stranger abduction. A few years later, reliable statistics showed that 99 percent of all child abductions annually were family-related.

Still, in 1984 *Newsweek* published a cover story with the words "Stolen Children" screaming from the stands. The article allowed that "90 to 95 percent [of children reported missing] are likely to be runaways or youngsters abducted by a parent involved in a custody fight." It also managed the rhetorical feat of suggesting that the visceral impact of the rare cases was enough to effectively render them the rule rather than the exception. "Though they constitute the smallest portion of the missing-children phenomenon," the reporter wrote, "they can be weighted at ten times their number for the emotional havoc they leave in their wake."

It's always seemed to me no accident that the panic over kidnappings in the 1980s—as well as the panic over

satanic-cult members molesting preschoolers, which happened around the same time—coincided with masses of
middle-class women, many of them mothers, returning to or
entering the workplace. What better way to punish women
for breaking free from the housewife mold than to reimagine
children as a victimized class? After centuries (millennia?)
of playing outdoors alone and generally being left to their
own devices, children who came home to empty houses now
fell into a woebegotten category called latchkey kids, their
house keys hanging from shoestrings around their necks
like scarlet letters. But even as these unsupervised urchins
haunted the public imagination, the threats to them were
just that, imaginary. Working moms weren't just the scape-
goats of these threats, but, often, the target audience for the
doomsaying. It was a perfect marketing ploy. Who could be
the more ideal viewer for those requisite yearly news stories
about razor blades stuck in Halloween candy than moms
too busy working outside the home to sew homemade costumes? (Did you know that kids with store-bought costumes
are disproportionately poisoned by anthrax-laced Snickers
bars? No, you didn't, because it's not true. Nor has there ever
been a single documented case of a stranger poisoning trick-
or-treaters' candy.)

Moral panics can frequently be traced back to the dis-
comforts brought about by social change. With the invention
of electricity came fears that lights inside houses at nighttime
would alert intruders as to whether people were home. In
the 1950s, when films and musicals like *Rebel Without a Cause*

and *West Side Story* made teenage gangs into a cultural trope, everyone suddenly became afraid of switchblades and federal laws were proposed to ban them. Since then, we've been told that the population is under threat from everything from video games to juvenile "super-predators" to the idea that the United States is rife with child sex trafficking (a claim often made by those wanting to see punitive measures taken against adult sex workers). Today, social media can take a random conspiracy theory or misreported fact and turn it into a population-wide anxiety attack in a matter of hours. So, in the scheme of things, stranger-danger panic may look like just another entry in the Encyclopedia of Problems People Invent in Order to Distract Themselves from Their Actual Problems.

But stranger-danger panic always seemed to me to follow a particularly cynical and shameful logic, since it ignored the fact that less affluent mothers had been going to work for decades, though apparently to such little notice that no one bothered to poison any Halloween candy in retribution. Only when middle-class, college-educated types (the kind who might write *Newsweek* headlines or be on intimate terms with those who do) joined the fray did the official backlash begin. Only when women began encroaching on spaces where there was real money to be made and real agency to be gained were we suddenly notified of a pandemic of child peril. Inevitably, it became a self-fulfilling prophecy. Thirty years later, children are more fussed over than ever, dulled by psychotropic medication and so lulled by technology that many parents can't get their kids to play outside if they try. This, in turn, has become its own moral panic. *Newsweek* may have lost most of its currency, but type "coddled child" into Google and you'll get about nine thousand results (type it in without the quotations marks and you'll get more than half a million).

I'm not going to do a retread of the coddled-children phenomenon here. Yes, I do think kids in the middle and upper-middle classes are often over-entwined with their parents. But I have plenty of friends who are epic coddlers of their children, and I respect them enough to assume they have their reasons. As a non-parent, I know my thoughts on the matter are of limited interest or relevance. Moreover, the subject has been so hashed out during the last several years that it's no longer a hash as much as a pitifully weak sauce that gets poured onto every discussion about *why young people are the way they are*. But in thinking back on my own childhood, I'm struck mainly not by how coddled or uncoddled I was but how eager I was to grow up. Much as I enjoyed playing with my gender-neutral toys and watching *Zoom* and imitating Jodie Foster in *Freaky Friday*, I would have gladly dispensed with all of it in exchange for an express ticket to adulthood. There was something about childhood that was almost insulting. Being treated as fragile, vulnerable, and incapable of making decisions felt like a gross injustice. (If at ten years old I'd been proficient in the idiom of today's social justice activism, I might have even called it "a violence.")

Of course, I *was* fragile and vulnerable in some ways and definitely incapable of making certain decisions (given the opportunity to choose a name for a younger sibling, I might have suggested Holidome). But the best thing about being a kid, as far as I was concerned, was that it was a temporary situation.

More than forty years have passed since that awkward encounter with the chivalrous boy at the pool. I am far older now than my mother was back then. I'm even far older than she was in 1982, when we heard the news about the ERA being dead for good. In that time, the earnestness of my mother's feminism has done a reverse-pike dive into the irony of third-wave feminism. Gloria Steinem's "This Is What a Feminist Looks Like" shirt is back in style and available in countless Etsy stores in every imaginable color (right alongside all those "Don't Give a Fuck" T-shirts). But even more fashionable are T-shirts, plate necklaces, and coffee mugs reading "Feminist as Fuck." Slogans that were considered edgy in the 1970s, such as "Ladies Sewing Circle and Terrorist Society," which appeared on a shirt issued by the Oregon Women's Political Caucus in 1974, now seem banal compared to "I Drink Male Tears," "Kill All Men," "Pussy Grabs Back," or "My Feminism Will Be Intersectional or It Will Be Bullshit."

Is *this* what a feminist looks like?

Maybe it is, and maybe we should be glad. After all, it wasn't so many years ago, the mid-aughts, that female "empowerment" became strangely wrapped up in the culture of pornography and *Girls Gone Wild* videos. It seems like yesterday that female celebrities, when asked how they felt about the state of women, began their answers with "I'm not a feminist, but . . ." In the scheme of things, I suppose a runway model wearing a $700 Christian Dior "We Should All Be Feminists" T-shirt is no more perverse than women flashing their breasts in the name of reappropriating the forces of their sexual exploitation.

But I'm troubled by the ways in which contemporary feminism has turned womanhood into another kind of childhood, one inculcated with the same kind of fear and paranoia that haunted the children of the 1980s. Instead of milk cartons, we have news headlines. Every morning I wake up, pour my coffee, and click through news sites that are apparently determined to make every fourth story a jeremiad about the ways in which women are screwed. "Climate change 'impacts women more than men'" went a BBC headline in March 2018. "Men Have No Friends and Women Bear the Burden" was the title of a *Harper's Bazaar* article this past May.

Sometimes these are cases of headlines designed to provoke more outrage than anything actually contained in the accompanying article. The climate change story was essentially making the case that poor people are most affected by climate change and since women are poorer than men worldwide, well . . . ergo. The "men have no friends" story was mostly about how men can lean too heavily on their female partners because of stigmas against men seeking emotional support from other men. That's a phenomenon I have witnessed (though I've also noticed that women can wield a lot of power over emotionally dependent men), so the argument is fair enough, I suppose. But did the article really warrant a sub-headline that read: "Toxic masculinity—and the persistent idea that feelings are a 'female thing'—has left a generation of straight men stranded on an emotionally stunted island, unable to forge intimate relationships with other men. It's women who are paying the price"?

That was clearly the work of an editor seeking eyeballs by inserting buzzy terms like "toxic masculinity." (Well done! It caught my eye.) But in cases like the climate change article, such efforts aren't even necessary because the story is so easily massaged into a rote social justice narrative. Occasionally there's no massaging necessary because the story itself *is* the narrative. A recent standout in my feed was this: "Experts Say U.S. Among Ten Most Dangerous Nations for Women."

You read that right. A 2018 Thomson Reuters Foundation survey of "about 550 experts in women's issues" came up with a list of the ten countries in which women encountered the greatest risk of sexual violence, harassment, and coercion. The list included places like India, where gang rapes occur in public routinely and women, including very young girls, have been raped and set on fire, and countries like Afghanistan, Syria, Yemen, and Somalia, which are homes to honor killings, female genital mutilation, forced marriages, and any number of other atrocities imposed on women.

When asked why this was, the Thomson Reuters Foundation cited increased awareness of the issue thanks to the influence of the #MeToo movement.

"People want to think income means you're protected from misogyny, and sadly that's not the case," said one such expert by way of explanation. "We are going to look back and see this as a very powerful tipping point. . . . We're blowing the lid off and saying '#Metoo and Time's Up.'"

I guess "increased awareness" now counts as some kind of data point. Perception can now be interchangeable with fact. It's Etan Patz on the milk carton all over again. Wake up to this grim news every morning, year after year, and you'll start to believe it. Either that, or you'll start to think feminism itself is a moral panic.

Let's face it, though, in many ways, mother nature is the ultimate misogynist. There are real burdens to inhabiting a female body. It's a burden to walk down the street in that body, a burden to grow another body inside of that body. It's a burden to try to maintain equal footing with men when certain physical tasks we're less likely to be capable of—operating a pump on an oil rig, picking up steel beams, being seven feet tall and putting a ball through a hoop—have, fairly or unfairly, been assigned a higher monetary value than physical tasks like, say, bearing children. It's a burden to worry about getting pregnant when you don't want to be and not being able to get pregnant when you do. It's a burden—not to mention infuriating—to watch socially conservative lawmakers try to manage their own sexual demons and clusterfucked value systems by policing the rights of others.

It's also easy for Gen Xers and baby boomers to over-look the ways in which younger generations might experience those burdens more palpably. Data suggests that millennials, for all their sexting and Snapchat exhibitionism, have less sex than any generation since the 1920s. Research conducted by psychologist Jean Twenge, who studies generational differences, found that 15 percent of twenty- to twenty-four-year-olds who were born in the 1990s had not had a sexual partner since the age of eighteen. Gen Xers were two and a half times more likely to have been sexually active in their twenties than today's twentysomethings.

Though the exact reasons for this are difficult to quantify, Twenge has surmised that easy access to pornography plays a role, as does the fact that so much socializing is done online. And though my own theories are even more difficult to quantify, I'll nonetheless offer up one of them: when you come of age experiencing sex primarily through the filter of screens, the real thing must seem pretty scary. Moreover, if much of your sex education has come via the virtual classroom of internet pornography, it must be easy to get the idea that sex is more of a performative act than a natural function, a simulacrum of pleasure rather than pleasure itself.

How can that not contribute to the proliferation of nude selfies? How can it not affect notions of consent, of intimacy, of beauty, of physical adult realities like body hair? (And not for the better, since being programmed to recoil in disgust at the sight of body hair is hardly an evolutionary advantage; if the cavemen had been sticklers for the shaved look, we would all have died out twenty thousand years ago.) If I'd grown up with the idea that men would be repelled by me unless my entire body was as hairless as a mole rat (for much of the aughts, this was the standard for women), I might have wanted to #KillAllMen, too.

So I get it that I don't totally get it.

But what I think I'm justified in not understanding is what women stand to gain by reinforcing a narrative that they are a persecuted group. Even more so, what possible use is there in furthering the notion that to be a hip and cool feminist today means you can reduce men to insulting stereotypes in order to, in some sense, beat them at their own assholic game? Even before the election of the pussy grabber in chief, even before the #MeToo movement came along, there was a sense that feminism now existed as a response to some sort of emergency. But what exactly was the emergency? And how much of it was confined to online spaces as opposed to the real world? The idea of passive sexism, which could mean anything from a man holding a door for a woman to a school nurse calling a sick child's mother instead of his father, was suddenly on radar screens, and there was an entire genre of online journalism devoted to calling it out, the conclusion often being that "the world hates women." These journalists were then subjected to the sort of invective that opinion journalists have received for as long as there has been opinion writing. That is to say, they were called stupid, ugly, and unworthy of their jobs. Sometimes they got rape and death threats. Having been on the receiving end of some of that myself, my takeaway was usually that the world hates opinion journalists. But for others, the invective served to prove their point that the world hates women.

This feminism doesn't look like my feminism. Too often, it looks like some desperate overcompensation. It looks like narcissism repackaged as revolution. I'll just say it. The pussy hats at the Women's March made me cringe a little. So did the "Fuck" signs and the "Nasty Woman" shirts and the ovary sweaters and the vulva costumes. I acknowledge that those images got disproportionate play in the media. I confess that I didn't actually attend the 2017 march. If I'd been in New York or any other big city, I would have been there in a second, but it happened that I'd just arrived in Iowa City for a teaching stint and would have had to make a solo trip to Des Moines to attend the nearest march of any size. (Let the record show that the night before the march I attended a fundraiser for an Iowa City abortion clinic.) I know that what I was seeing in news clips didn't tell the whole story. Still, some of the cruder optics disappointed me, partly because so much of the rest of the march made me swell with hope. The sheer numbers—half a million or more in Washington, 400,000 in New York City, 500,000 in Los Angeles, even thousands in places like Boise and Spokane and Tulsa—suggested somehow that the election had been a big mistake, a simple misunderstanding; if this many people turned out in the freezing cold to register disapproval for what had just happened, then surely it wouldn't be happening for very long.

But, as I saw it, the theatrical crudeness that showed up

in media images in outsize proportions threatened the seriousness of the project. The message of the protests—that the election had not just been stolen from Clinton but violently mugged from her—felt so obvious, so unassailable, so much like a moral slam dunk, that undermining it with pussy hats felt self-sabotaging, like entering a race you're all but guaranteed to win but getting disqualified on a wardrobe technicality. In a radio interview I listened to, a Republican lawmaker was asked about the Women's March. When he said he could find nothing to criticize about it other than the profanity-laden signage, I thought about how nice it would have been if he didn't even have that to criticize. I thought about how nice it would be if people were still getting excited about Michelle Obama's "When they go low, we go high" line from the previous summer.

If you want to accuse me of peddling respectability politics, I won't argue with you. I appreciate respectability politics as a strategy. In 2018, especially during the awful summer where we saw the beginnings of border separations and immigrant children kept in cages, there was a lot of arguing going on as to whether the time for civility in the Trump resistance was up. The logic was that putting kids in cages was so egregious that the only appropriate response was "Fuck you, fuck you, fuck you!" Some liberals, myself among them, suggested that unrelenting outrage, including indiscriminately calling people Nazis, served only to alienate people who might finally be ready to leave the dark side. Others maintained that anything less than around-the-clock outrage, even when it seemed unhinged, was morally unconscionable. A year later, though I still err on the side of the civility camp, I can see both sides.

But in January of 2017, when the shock was still setting in, I found myself wishing everyone would shut up, button up, and register their dissent without being so potty-mouthed about it. I found myself perversely (irrationally, ridiculously) wishing that all the protesters could have worn some kind of, I don't know . . . *uniform*? Perhaps they could have sheathed themselves in American flags or dressed up as bald eagle mascots. (Imagine the aerial shots!) I wished we could have given the enemy no opportunity to feel anything but shame.

During that time, I found myself drawing upon images from the Freedom Rides and lunch-counter sit-ins of the early civil rights era. No doubt I was falling prey to false nostalgia and the distorting, romanticizing effects of old photographs and archival film footage, but the differences between then and now were striking. You saw men in jackets and ties and women in dresses. You saw perfectly comported young black people sitting at lunch counters reading books while white men jeered at them and looked idiotic for doing so.

"Their leaders . . . were doing what many leaders routinely do," the black legal scholar Randall Kennedy wrote in a *Harper's* essay defending respectability politics from a progressive position, "packaging their campaigns in ways designed to blunt the opposition of their enemies, to elicit solidarity from supporters, and to induce acceptance from the uncommitted."

Should women do some version of this? Could we? Is it possible that we could all put on smart-looking blazers and march through the streets holding signs that make our point a way that is concise and clever but doesn't compromise our dignity? Is it unreasonable to expect 51 percent of the human population to agree on a single definition of dignity so as to blunt the opposition of our enemies through the sheer force of it?

Even back in Martin Luther King's day, despite the jackets and ties, there was little agreement about this. During the summer of 2018 I thought a lot about King's condemnation of the white moderate in "Letter from a Birmingham Jail." I thought about how King called this moderate the "great stumbling block in the stride toward freedom," notably for the moderate's milquetoast appeal of "I agree with you in the goal you seek, but I can't agree with your methods of direct action."

I am the white feminist version of this white moderate. (Make that white, Gen X, stick-in-the-mud contrarian feminist version.) I am the feminist who gets accused of "pearl clutching" in response to flagrant and reflexive uses of the word "fuck" and endless repeats of the word "vagina." I don't own a pair of pearls. But I'll tell you why this vernacular makes me cringe. It's not that it's embarrassing as much as it's a way of gesturing at being radical without really being radical at all. It's a kind of shorthand edginess, which means it's a shortcut *to* edginess. It's essentially the ideological version of buying the Ramones' *Hey Ho Let's Go: Greatest Hits* and no other Ramones records and still calling yourself the biggest Ramones fan in the world. Saying "fuck" all the time is meant to convey a resistance to stuffy idiomatic convention. Saying "vagina" again and again is meant to convey body positivity; it's a standoff with shame. Or at least it's supposed to be. More often it isn't. Saying these words all the time doesn't convey edginess as much as lack of imagination. Posting "fuck Trump" on Facebook every five minutes doesn't convey political resistance as much as verbal atrophy. Calling yourself a badass doesn't convey anything other than the distinct impression that you are, in fact, the opposite of a badass.

Let's consider the case—or at least the memeification—of the badass for a moment. The badass is—and in many ways remains—the face of fourth-wave feminist sanctimonium, the symbol of all that is righteous and unassailable about modern womanhood. She is the state-of-the-art version of liberated femaleness, the ne plus ultra of self-sovereignty and zero fuck giving. The best thing about the badass club is that just about any female possessed of a scintilla of self-sufficiency can qualify. Once upon a time, when the word was rarely used, you more or less had to escape captivity in North Korea or sit in a Greenpeace raft in the Southern Ocean facing down the harpoon of a Japanese whaling ship in order to be designated a badass. Today, no such bells and whistles are required. A woman need only take it upon herself to educate a man on the ways in which he is mansplaining, wear a "Nasty Woman" T-shirt, or just say the word "vagina" a lot, and she, too, will be conferred badass status.

If that's still too much, it's entirely acceptable to just proclaim yourself a badass and be done with it. This can be accomplished on Twitter with a #badass hashtag—"Sometimes just getting through the day as a woman feels like competing in an Ironman triathlon #badass"—or in real life by looking in the mirror and congratulating yourself for holding down a job or paying your rent on time. Because, Lord knows, getting out of bed and going to work every day requires more than just a modicum of personal drive; it means facing down the patriarchy at every turn.

There are at least two major categories of badass. There's the hip indie version and the slick corporate version. Like the word "feminist" itself, "badass" has been sanitized, branded, and commodified. It can now be found on coffee mugs and key chains, and as entire boards on the kinds of Pinterest accounts that also have boards for skinny jeans and nameplate necklaces ("badass" itself being an especially popular name on such plates). I would not be at all surprised to sort through the offerings at a fitness-studio boutique and find, among workout clothing bearing phrases like "Spiritual Gangster," an $80 tank top reading "Badass." The author Jen Sincero has a massively successful franchise built around her breakout self-help book, *You Are a Badass*, which admittedly I read one night in a single sitting and then lay awake for hours in a kind of sugar coma of amorphous ambition to change my life. (I awoke the next morning so sleepy that I hit the snooze button several times before finally rising from my perpetually unmade bed and facing my perpetually unchanged life.)

When they are not opining on Twitter about the gender

wage gap or posting makeup-free ("because DGAF!") selfies on Instagram, badasses take to the streets. They pull out their phones and snap photos of men who take up too much room on subway seats, then post the photos on social networking accounts created for the very purpose of shaming such men. They capture video of street harassers, which they share on social media to a chorus of exuberant and indignant approval. They start Tumblr blogs like Straight White Boys Texting, which gathers particularly gross and inappropriate text messages from men (often in the context of dating apps) and displays them for badasses all over the world to see and pillory. If anyone suggests that this sort of mockery and dismissal amounts to sexism against men, they let out a collective howl of laughter in the form of "ironic misandry." That would include quips like "boys suck," "kill all men," and, most notably, "I bathe in male tears," a phrase that has made its way onto coffee mugs, T-shirts, and needlepoint pillows and has been called the contemporary version of the 1980s catchphrase "This is what a feminist looks like."

The "male tears" meme emerged sometime around 2012 as a response to men's rights activists who accused feminists of misandry, and the term gained further viral traction when feminist writer Jessica Valenti (who's technically a Gen Xer but has legions of millennial fans) fought back against some Twitter bullies by tweeting a photo of herself wearing a shirt that read "I bathe in male tears." The idea behind this meme is that it's not an earnest bashing of men but an in-joke among social-media-savvy women. It represents a kind of radical indifference to men and anyone else who just doesn't get it. Writing about this phenomenon in *Slate* in 2014, Amanda Hess conceded that she was "too shy for message T-shirts and too square for Instagram memes" but was still grateful to have ironic misandry as one of many tools for dealing with culturally ingrained misogyny.

"Some sexist provocations are too tiresome to counter with a full-throated feminist argument," Hess wrote. "Sometimes, all you need is a GIF."

Hess, who has written stories that I admire a great deal, is about fifteen years younger than I am. I couldn't agree more with the first sentence of that quote and couldn't agree less with the last. When it comes to tiresome sexist provocations, we'd all do well to shut our mouths and throats and (how's this for an idea?) our ears.

As I see it, the eye-roll GIF is the most cavalier and snot-nosed form of retort since "talk to the hand." If you disagree with someone on ideological grounds, the reasonable response is to either lay out your own argument or, if the provocation is indeed too tiresome, disengage altogether. Disengaging does not make you, as they say now, "complicit in oppression" (or, as we used to say, "part of the problem"). It suggests you have better things to do, which, let's face it, is the kind of suggestion that drives Twitter trolls and ideological opponents berserk. I can't for the life of me see why a GIF of Emma Stone rolling her eyes in disgust is considered a substitute for a counterargument. I don't see how saying "fuck" all the time makes you sound tough when it's actually laziness incarnate.

While we're here, let's talk about "fuck" for a moment. Any self-respecting badass knows that it's mandatory to use it, or some variation of it, at least every six and a half seconds. And why not? What an indispensable multitasker of a word it's become! No longer relegated to that marginalized category once known as profanity, "fuck" now wears many syntactical hats and is a staple of the badass vocabulary.

In addition to being a fun way to embed a little malediction into an otherwise austere word (see "patri-fucking-archy"), "fuck" is now a synonym for "care" ("care" as noun, that is, as in "having a care"). It achieved this status by passing through the ranks of interchangeability with "damn" and "shit" (as in "I don't give a ___"). As anyone can see, "damn" and "shit" used in this context are poor substitutes for the power and implied political wokeness of "fuck." Can you imagine if Rhett Butler had said to Scarlett O'Hara, "Frankly my dear, I don't give a fuck"? Instead of embodying the essence of toxic masculinity, he'd come across as a cool blogger. Or a person with a lot of Instagram followers—a fuckton of followers even.

To quote film critic Anthony Lane mocking Yoda's blathering New Age syntax in a review of *Star Wars: Episode III—Revenge of the Sith*, "Break me a fucking give."

This is not about me clutching my pearl necklace in horror over the use of "fuck." Like I said, I don't own a pearl necklace and, if you must know, most of my other necklaces are tangled together in a drawer because I'm still bad at being a girl and don't know how to properly store my jewelry. This is about the ways in which badass feminism feels, paradoxically, like a pink aisle at a toy store. It feels like a feminism that has been preselected for mass consumption, distributed by social media algorithms, and, above all, brilliantly engineered to tap into our most narcissistic weaknesses while masquerading as strength. Like those pink toys, it can make you feel a little sick even as you feel like part of the in-group. And, let's face it, no matter how much you think you're above such concerns, the desire to be—and to remain—in the in-group is still a driving force in female life.

I was bad at being a girl, and now I'm bad at being a woman. I don't do many of the things that women are supposed to do. Worse, I don't feel many of the things women are supposed to feel. Some of those things, like taking care of children—like feeling the desire to take care of children—are old news when it comes to feeling like you're doing things wrong. That's introductory-level Failing as a Woman, and I completed that course long ago (I'd like to think I got an A-plus, if that's not too oxymoronic). What I'm faced with now is a failure to be the right kind of feminist during a time when we're told we can't afford the wrong kind.

Where I have failed is that I'm not an emergency-response feminist. I am not wearing the ovary sweater and the pussy hat like flashing siren lights. I am not refraining from criticizing the #KillAllMen brigades on the grounds that there's a war going on and we can't afford any breaks in the ranks. Instead, I'm asking if this is really what feminism should look like. Are we really going about this the right way? Because I'm pretty sure it's not what my mother had in mind when she sat with me on the Texas Capitol steps that day. I'm pretty sure what she wanted for me was a world in which "free to be you and me" really meant something.

CHAPTER 3

....

Just Switch Chairs and Move On:
Fearless Girls at Work

For several years in my twenties I shared a rambling, roach-infested, but otherwise quite desirable apartment in New York City near Columbia University. There were three people in residence at any given time, and though we were usually all women, we had a handful of male roommates, too. Periodically someone would move out, and the remaining roommate and I would advertise for a replacement by stapling flyers onto telephone poles around the neighborhood. Competition was tough—the bedroom most often up for grabs rented for less than $500—and we usually set aside a day during which candidates would file in for interviews like actors on a casting call.

There was one applicant in particular I'll never forget. The year was 1995 or so, and the remaining roommate and I were both in graduate school and working any number of side hustles to pay the rent (I was registered with several temp agencies and routinely blew off my campus job to do secretarial work in Midtown offices, which paid twice as much). We probably interviewed a dozen candidates that day, most of them students or struggling artists or people in entry-level jobs—people a lot like us. One man who came was different. Balding and slightly stoop shouldered, he was probably in his thirties, but my roommate and I perceived him as dodderingly old. Eager to sell himself, he had a proposition for us.

"How about you girls do the cooking if I pay for the food?" he asked.

My roommate and I were afraid to even glance in the other's direction lest we make eye contact and collapse into fits of laughter.

Suffice it to say we were not offended. We were worried about offending *him* with our reflexive mockery. Was this because we were too blind to our own oppression to fully register his chauvinism? Hardly. It was because his chauvinism utterly disempowered him. He stood before us as a pathetic creature, a human-shaped dust bunny being swept, before our very eyes, into the trash bin of history. This had nothing to do, by the way, with being an adult in his thirties and needing to live with roommates (there is nothing remarkable about this in New York City). It was because his cluelessness rendered his attitudes and opinions irrelevant. He was totally not our problem.

If this had happened in 2015 rather than 1995, I suppose my roommate and I might have reacted differently. Maybe one of us would have made a beeline to her laptop and composed a rage-filled Tumblr post replete with hashtags like #Fuck-WhiteMen and #SmashThePatriarchy. Maybe we would have given our guest a steely reprimand, bid him adieu, and then retreated to the kitchen to pour vodka into our "Male Tears" coffee mugs. Surely, we would have been talking about this guy and his pitiful overture for days to anyone within earshot. After all, this was no mere microaggression but sexist piggery in its purest form, a scene from *Mad Men* come to life.

As it was, *Mad Men* was a decade away from appearing on our television screens. More importantly, decades had passed since this sort of behavior would have been commonplace, at least in our circles. Which is maybe why my roommate and I were essentially unfazed by it. We may have been caught off guard, but it was more like bumping into a relic of the past. It made us appreciate the present that much more.

We'd heard about men like this before, of course, mostly from our second-wave feminist mothers recounting what life had been like before the women's movement. As I think about this now, it occurs to me that our mothers would surely have been enraged at the idea of cooking for a male roommate because it would have seemed so plausible. Put the whole scenario in 1975 and it might look something like a pre-internet version of the 2015 scenario; there would be lecturing and fist shaking. There would be heavy emotional processing at a political action group.

Our mothers' mandate would have been to try to root out this kind of chauvinism and set history on a better course.

In 1995, our mandate was to laugh it out of the room. Our mothers had yelled, but we would snort. Men like these weren't threats to us. They were embarrassments to themselves. Their aggressions were neither personal nor political. They were just moronic.

This seems to me an entirely natural response to boorish male behavior. Strange as it may sound to say in today's climate, the concept of male privilege was largely alien to me at that time. From my earliest memories, the general vibe around boys was that they were inferior to girls. Boys couldn't sit still in class, couldn't read as well as girls, got in trouble more often, matured later, and, even then, never really seemed to catch up. Insofar as teachers called on boys more often than on girls in elementary school, my impression was always that the teachers were grateful that *any* boy had *anything* to say and called on them out of desperation. This was no doubt a product of my own blinkered upbringing. From an early age, I'd gravitated, or been pushed by my parents (there was always a fine line between my interests and theirs), toward arts-oriented, female-dominated pursuits like theater and orchestra. Boys here either existed on the sidelines or, in the case of high school theater, were in such short supply that simply showing up for an audition was enough to get a boy cast in a leading male part.

This pattern continued as I went to a female-dominated liberal arts college and then worked in the women's magazine business. My first job was at a fashion and beauty magazine, and though I scoffed at the essential shallowness of the enterprise, many of the women were absolute killers, sharks swimming in raging seas of haute couture and chemical facial peels. There were men sprinkled here and there, yet even the physical posture of these men suggested they lived perennially under the thumbs of women, like moss beneath toadstools. The women were buying their own apartments, trading their own stocks, out-earning their boyfriends and husbands. They also screamed at their assistants and threw small office supplies across the room. They connived, they berated, they mistreated their subordinates. There may have been more men than women at the very top of this food chain, but their presence felt almost symbolic, as if they were artists' renderings that just happened to be walking around in the world instead of confined to picture frames.

After that job, I went to a graduate school program where women not only outnumbered men but could be so ruthless in their critiques of certain men that, as in elementary school, the professors sometimes seemed to be favoring those men out of pity. Sure, a handful of my male classmates were the kind of patronizing, blowhard types that would now be referred to as mansplainers. Likewise, there were more than a handful of men in the publishing and media business—a world in which I was extremely eager to make my mark—that were more than happy to lord their influence over anyone they could, especially young women who could be taken out to lunches that, halfway through, began to feel strangely like dates, as I knew all too well. Beyond that, of course, there would always be men you crossed the street to avoid and men you didn't give your number to and plenty of reasons (all of them having to do with the animalistic opportunism of some males) not to leave your drink unattended in a bar.

But feeling the need to take such precautions seemed to be a different thing from feeling that men had power over me. If anything, the precautions were further proof of the ways in which the animal nature of men made them a lesser primate. Men such as the would-be roommate were on the verge of extinction. There was no need to make a fuss about them. As far as I could see, they'd be gone soon enough.

But that was just my experience. As was frequently the case in my twenties (and even today, though I try to do better) I couldn't see very far past the confines of my social bubble. While I was rolling my eyes at the pretentious ramblings of insecure dudes in my writing workshop, my good friend Eileen was in downtown Manhattan, at a Wall Street investment bank, cleaning semen off her desk. One morning in 1995 she arrived at work and discovered that someone had jerked off all over her workstation. She knew who'd done it. She also knew there was almost certainly video footage proving so, though when she went to security and reported that her desk had been "vandalized," she was told that no such tape existed. She didn't bother reporting it to a supervisor or anyone in human resources. In fact, she says she's not even sure this company had a human resources department.

"The guy was a high-producing stock trader," she told me. "No one was going to touch him."

By way of background, Eileen and I have been friends since

the sixth grade, though we were—and are—in many ways opposites. She was good at math and science, whereas I was so miserable in these areas that I once begged my geometry teacher to let me write a paper about Pythagoras of Samos just to get a passing grade (request denied: I wound up in summer school). Eileen, who would be the first in her family to go to college and knew she needed scholarships to get there, was focused on getting good grades and high test scores and, above all, setting herself up for a remunerative career. I, on the other hand, obsessively pursued the things that interested me (writing, drama, orchestra) and effectively ignored everything else.

Eileen and I both went to Seven Sisters colleges, she to Wellesley and me to Vassar. But whereas she majored in economics and secured herself a solid boyfriend from a neighboring university, I cultivated an air of bohemian pretentiousness that prepared me for little more than a life of the same. After college, Eileen got engaged to the solid boyfriend at what I thought was the scandalously young age of twenty-five. More than two decades later, Eileen pretty much has the best marriage of anyone I know.

There were framed photos of Eileen's fiancé on her desk when the trader, shall we say, liquidated his holdings all over it. Along the way, the trader had knocked the photos to the ground and just generally ransacked the surface of her desk.

"He was a paranoid guy," Eileen told me on the phone more than twenty years after the incident. (We weren't in frequent enough contact back in the day for her to have told me about it then.) "He was in over his head, constantly thinking he was going to lose money. He probably had a crush on me. He never approached me directly or talked to me. My guess is that he had some repressed thing."

I asked if she reported the incident to a manager or some authoritative body.

"I didn't report it," she said. "If you're going to report that kind of thing, you know you're risking your job. Not to mention your future jobs. No one wants to be known as 'the woman whose desk got jacked off on.'"

Several things occurred to me during this conversation. The first was the girl-power bubble in which I've spent my career is perhaps not the most useful perch from which to make pronouncements about the death of the patriarchy. The exultant image of Melanie Griffith riding the Staten Island Ferry to corporate triumph in the 1988 film *Working Girl* may be permanently tattooed on my emotional memory card (and in a very positive way), but the truth is that Wall Street was and is a hostile place for women—much more so than I'd realized. The desk incident may have been the most egregious of the indignities Eileen endured, but there were also drunken boob grabs at parties and raucous (also drunken) parties where Eileen was publicly berated as though the subject of a roast.

"It would start out as teasing me for being a prude, being a Goody Two-Shoes," she recalls about the roasting, "but it would quickly escalate into outright hostility."

Aside from being forced to reckon with my naivete, what really struck me about our conversation is the way Eileen talked about her . . . what should we call him? Second-degree

assailant? Vandal? Walking biohazard? She spoke of him almost with an air of pity. He was paranoid, in over his head,
repressed in his feelings for her and/or women in general. She
did not talk, then or now, about rape culture or toxic masculinity. Not once did she say she felt unsafe. Though she was
the only woman in her department who wasn't a secretary, she
was quick to point out that by and large she felt supported by
her male colleagues. She worked in research, "where all the
geeks were," she told me. "They were kinder and had more ca-
maraderie." When she brought a coworker over to her desk to
show him what had happened, the coworker registered sympathy with a roll of the eyes.

"He said something like 'Ugh, that's bad,'" she recalled,
laughing. "He found me a new chair. He wasn't exactly part of
the male-bravado thing there. He said, 'Just switch chairs and
move on.'"

Just switch chairs and move on. That sounds like a reaction
GIF in the making, perhaps a 2.0 version of that omnipres-
ent "Keep Calm and Carry On" poster. Except it's not the
kind of sentiment that gains a lot of traction in this era of
performed outrage. Talking with Eileen, I couldn't help but
think of *Fearless Girl*, the bronze statue created by sculptor
Kristen Visbal that appeared in Manhattan's Financial District in the spring of 2017. Depicting a spunky-looking,
ponytailed little girl with her hands placed defiantly on her
hips, the statue was commissioned by an investment firm

and placed in Bowling Green in front of the famous 7,000-pound *Charging Bull* sculpture outside the New York Stock Exchange.

Instantly, that statue became a repository for every possible iteration of feminist and capitalist critique—not to mention art commentary. Since it had been installed overnight just before International Women's Day (not that this holiday is observed by your average passerby), the surface-level message was one of female resistance to male authoritarianism. But despite the investment firm's statement that the statue represented "the power of women in leadership," naysayers almost immediately began pointing out that the company employed very few female executives. Furthermore, the company had recently settled a lawsuit admitting they had fraudulently charged secret markups for services. Therefore *Fearless Girl* amounted to nothing more than a conciliatory distraction device.

More controversy burbled up from there. Some adult women didn't like that their achievements were being represented by a child. In yet another wrinkle, Arturo Di Modica, the artist who created *Charging Bull*, complained that the new visual narrative suggested that *Fearless Girl* was facing down the bull and that this subverted the meaning of his statue. The bull, he said, was meant to symbolize "freedom in the world, peace, strength, power, and love." Others saw the bull as symbolizing the vigor of an upward-trending bull market. Whatever the case, the bull was never supposed to connote the bullying nature of men—at least not until it came face-to-face with a statue of a little girl.

There was also this: days after *Fearless Girl* went up, a young man in a suit, a prototypical-looking Wall Street bro, was caught in a photo rubbing up against the statue simulating a sex act. Naturally, the image went viral, and, naturally, an avalanche of outrage came along for the ride. "Man in Suit Humping 'Fearless Girl' Statue Is Why We Need Feminism" was the *Huffington Post* headline. My Twitter feed was a chorus singing in unison: *Another day in rape culture. It just never stops. As if we needed more evidence that the world hates women.*

The perpetrator's face was blurry in the photo, but he seemed easily identifiable nonetheless. In anticipatory schadenfreude, I kept waiting for his name to be made public and for his incarceration in the digital stockade to begin. Amazingly, it never did. Meanwhile, I actually began to wonder if the whole incident wasn't in some way another day in rape-culture *resistance*. The offending bro (who, according to bystanders, had been hanging off the bull statue with his buddies moments earlier) managed to defile *Fearless Girl* for only a few seconds before horrified bystanders shouted him off. Then he was forced into hiding by the angry internet mob. Not only was he castigated for his crime, he kept the feminist conversation's volume on high for another day—or three. Is this evidence that the world hates women? Or just further proof of the infantile, psychologically impotent nature of Wall Street bros? Would an equally accurate headline have been "Outrage at Man in Suit Humping 'Fearless Girl' Statue Is Why Feminism Is Winning"?

Here's another possible headline: "Man in Suit Humping

'Fearless Girl' Statue Is 2017 Version of Man Ejaculating on Woman's Desk in 1995 and the Fact That He Was Shamed Instead of Ignored Is Why Feminism Is Winning."

If something like the desk incident had happened today, Eileen told me, she probably would have taken photos. But of course that was in the days before smartphones effectively became extensions of people's hands. Besides, even if she had been able to take photos and march into HR and somehow get the guy fired by noon, this would have done little to save her from a fate of being forever known as "the woman whose desk got jacked off on." As it happens, years later, at another job, not in finance but a very corporate setting nonetheless, Eileen experienced sexual harassment and did attempt to report it. She retained a lawyer (a woman, incidentally) and was told she had no evidence and therefore no case. As much of a minefield as that work environment was, she says it still had nothing on Wall Street. She also says she wouldn't trade the Wall Street experience for anything.

"I'm glad I did it," Eileen told me. "All the stuff that happened to me, it's all life experience. It has value, even if it was miserable at the time. That said, if it were my daughter in that situation I'd tell her to get the fuck out of there."

I don't need to have kids to know exactly what she means.

Much of life is a process of knowing when and if to get out of one situation or another. I've spent a lot of time over the last few years thinking about where I went wrong versus where I was perhaps done wrong. It can be difficult to separate the two under any circumstances. But when you find yourself getting divorced and stepping squarely into middle age amid a cultural referendum on the treatment and value of women, you can't help but make a case study of yourself. *Women are so aggrieved right now,* I'd think while driving around with my dog during our weekly adventures in moving the car on alternate side of the street parking days. *What are my grievances? What have been the times in my life where male privilege has blocked my way?*

Maybe it's my natural temperament (and maybe this is proof that my temperament is fundamentally narcissistic), but there's no one I'd rather blame for my misfortunes than myself. In a pinch, I'll blame the whims of the universe, but for the most part I'll never pass up an opportunity for self-admonition. This is especially true when it comes to grievances against men and male privilege, which I take a special delight in quashing in favor of my own accountability. It's almost as if blaming myself strips the men of their power by rendering them too insignificant to even gripe about.

In the eighth grade I ran for student body president against the most popular guy in the entire junior high school. One afternoon, as I was organizing my locker, my opponent's football-player pals set upon me like a bunch of goons, encouraging me to run for student body secretary instead. The exact reason they gave now escapes me (probably it was something as convincing as "Steve really wants to be president"), but what doesn't escape me is how easily I caved to their request. I did so not because I knew Steve would beat me (he wouldn't have, because, as his goons were well aware, I would capture the "nerd vote") but because I was an idiotic fourteen-year-old girl and wanted Steve to like me. And in fact I did run for secretary (my campaign slogan: "Vote for Meghan: The Write Choice!") and won easily and served on the cabinet alongside Steve, who proved to be a very amiable and collaborative colleague.

An obvious narrative here would be that my eighth-grade political ambitions were felled by the patriarchy. It wasn't just that Steve was exhibiting sexism by assuming, consciously or not, that he, as a male, was more entitled to be president than I was. It was that, in placing more value on winning Steve's approval than winning the presidency, I was responding to culturally enforced patriarchal norms. So insidious were these norms that no amount of *Zoom* or *Free to Be . . . You and Me* or Jodie Foster fan worship in childhood could protect me. My feminist mother was undoubtedly disappointed by my capitulation. She registered her disapproval to me in measured tones before getting on the phone with her League of Women Voters friends and ranting about the backward nature of the whole school system and town. But this was not enough to throw me off my newly forged secretarial course. In my mind at the time, serving as class secretary alongside President Steve was a double achievement. It showed I was formidable enough to get voted into office but not so threatening as to be president or anything like that.

That's a sad story, I suppose. It's a story that, when subjected to the expected interpretation, perfectly telegraphs the ingrained sexism and internalized misogyny that keeps women off the top rungs of the ladder. It hints at just how impossible Hillary Clinton's task was when she ran for president; she had to win the nerd vote while also appeasing the football players. She had to convince people that it's possible to be the leader of the free world without being threatening. But just as I think gender alone doesn't account for Clinton's downfall, I've never been able to blame the patriarchy for thwarting my eighth-grade presidential run. Nor could I have blamed internalized misogyny even if that term had been around back then. It was more like internalized stupidity. Or Suburbia Induced Mediocrity Syndrome. Whatever it was, the decision I made was mine alone. There were probably any number of other girls who, had they wanted to run for president, would have had the strength of character to swat away Steve's henchmen as though they were common houseflies. (Not that these sorts of girls would have bothered to run for student council in the first place, since they would have probably lacked that need-to-be-liked gene that compels many people to run for any political office.)

Moreover, there were probably any number of eighth-grade girls who could have thrown me off my game by challenging me directly in a run for president. In all honesty, if some extremely popular girl had let it be known that she'd be my best friend if only I removed myself from the field of competitors, I may have taken her up on it. That's because for all my moxie, I was still in the eighth grade. My chief aspiration was to fit in and be liked. There are many ways in which that is still my chief aspiration.

I carried that aspiration with me on both shoulders through high school and college and into early adulthood, where somewhere along the way it shifted over to only my left shoulder. On my right shoulder is the antipode of this aspiration, the impulse to say what I really think and do what I really want even if it gets me a little cast out or a little (or a lot) disliked. All of the things I've done right—my best writing, my best relationships, the best places I've lived—have come from leading with my right shoulder. Everything I've gotten wrong, including the times when it could be said that I've been *done wrong* by someone, have come from leading with the left shoulder. I naturally favor the right, but only slightly.

All this is to say that it's difficult for me to think about grievance, especially toward men, in the way we're now supposed to think about it. And that is to say the search for grievance has become a kind of political obligation, an activist gesture—or at least something that passes for one. I remember sitting at my computer one morning reading with fascination a couple of Facebook posts by the same woman. The first was a magazine article about a successful female television showrunner in Hollywood. The article emphasized the sexism the showrunner encountered in the early years of her career, and the Facebook poster took the opportunity to share her own brief experience as a writer's assistant and the crude, bro-ish male behavior she endured from overwhelmingly male colleagues. Her comment was met instantly with the predictable cascade of affirmations and commiserations: *I. Can't. Even. Is this shit ever gonna get old? Bet they knew you were more talented and just couldn't handle it.*

Directly under this post was another from the same woman a few days earlier. This time it was a complaint about men not paying on dates. *When the check comes, you slap your credit card down right away*, she intoned, taking on the voice of a friendly if peeved advice giver to hapless single men. *Don't fuck it up and let the check sit there so she's forced to ask, "Should we split it?" It's the fastest way to emasculate yourself, turn us dry.*

Staring at my screen, I was awash in thoughts, most of which caved in on themselves through sheer force of their contradictions. On the one hand, I was well aware that men in Hollywood writers' rooms can be infantile, depraved pigs. I knew countless women who'd told me the same kinds of stories. I'd also been in enough Hollywood pitch meetings to see that many of the men who wind up in positions of power in that business are former teenage nerds attempting to make up for lost time by mistreating, rejecting, objectifying, or just generally being assholes to the kinds of women (in some cases all women) who wouldn't give them the time of day in high school. On the other hand, I happened to have read the article in question. It seemed clear the television creator had an unusual, even sometimes puzzling, style of going about her job. She seemed like an exceptionally cool person but also a notably unusual one. This made me wonder how much of the derision she sometimes faced was the result of sexism and how much was the result of her just being kind of weird to deal with.

More than that, though, I wondered why the writer of the article, a seasoned pro who no doubt knew what she was doing, had chosen to underscore the sexism factor. Was this just part and parcel of any discussion of a woman who has achieved high levels of professional success in a field that hasn't traditionally been dominated by women? Or was it in fact completely relevant because, weird and grating as this show creator's personality might be, male show creators can be equally weird and grating, if not more so, and no one would reject them out of hand for being difficult to work with? As I thought about it, it seemed clear that both things were true at once. Yes, the television creator had been subject to judgment in ways her male peers probably had not. And, yes, in pursuit of the sexism angle, the writer of the article had indulged in a rather perfunctory and probably needless checking off of boxes.

But then again, was it needless? Maybe it was the best angle after all. As I got up from my desk and went to the kitchen for more coffee, I found myself stewing in my own interrogative juices. The sexism angle irritated me for some reason, but maybe I was wrong to be irritated. After all, how often do male creatives get thrown under the bus because they're too difficult? Perhaps not that often. Was Francis Ford Coppola fired when the chaos of his set coincided with Martin Sheen suffering a heart attack during the filming of *Apocalypse Now*? Was David O. Russell's career ruined after a video of him exploding on set and hurling expletives at actors—including the beloved Lily Tomlin, of all people!—went viral? A woman in Coppola's shoes would have been deemed incompetent. A woman in Russell's shoes would be declared mentally ill, too big of an insurance risk to put on a set. How was this not proof of sexism? And why shouldn't the magazine writer have put it in the foreground of the article?

Overwhelmed by these questions, I moved on to the Facebooker's second gripe, about men not paying the bill on dates. Until a few months earlier, that issue would have been of little interest to me, but as it happened I had recently found myself wandering into the postdivorce dating arena on errant occasions. When I say "wandering," I mean it in the sense of accidentally deviating from my path into hostile territory, the way I sometimes nonsensically but also vividly imagine a tourist in South Korea might lean slightly in the wrong direction and wind up in North Korea and from there in a labor camp for life. I mean that I'd been on perhaps four dates with four different men at that point (I hadn't liked any of them enough to go on a second date). Some of these dates had ended in a sort of cordially tacit agreement that we'd split the bill. In no cases had that lessened my attraction to the men in question, mostly because I was attracted to so few of them in the first place.

I thought about all of this as I read the comments responding to the Facebook post, an alarming number of which were from women referring to the men on dating apps as "garbage." One woman bristled about how a man had made her pay for her drinks and then had the nerve to try to kiss her afterward. Another chimed in with a quip about the gender wage gap: *Come talk to us when women aren't earning $.79 for every dollar a man earns.*

I wasn't sure how old the original poster was—I wasn't sure how I was even connected to her in the first place—but it was clear she was younger and in a different phase of life than I was. It was clear she was looking for a serious commitment, which meant her dating stakes were exponentially higher than mine. While I was looking mostly to cleanse my palate after a complicated, loving, but also sadder-than-it-should-have-been marriage, she was looking for a life partner. While I was mostly delighted to be living alone again, leisurely grazing for meals rather than planning them, coming home to an empty apartment that didn't resent me for being out late, she was probably exhausted by the same. While I had hard proof that good men are out there, since I'd managed to marry one, she probably had no reason to believe the world wasn't populated by cheapskate "garbage" masquerading as eligible bachelors. I certainly hadn't when I was on the tenterhook that is singledom in your mid- to late thirties.

I didn't have to contend with dating apps, either. Or even regular online dating. (I actually met men in real-life situations like parties or the library, a feat I now look on with the same astonishment I feel about once being able to do a backflip.) I didn't have the opportunity to lay my soul bare on social media in exchange for cheap solidarity. I didn't have in my constant sight line a thousand web magazines and Tumblr sites reminding me what was wrong with the world in general and how I was getting screwed specifically. If these things had existed in my younger days, perhaps I would have been coming home from disappointing dates and letting my frustrations rip on Facebook. As it was, I phoned my friends late at night and vented my frustrations at them.

Was that really any different from what this Facebooker was doing? During the first few years of my postdivorce life, I spent a lot of time observing what had changed over the decade or so since I'd last been single. A decade isn't so long in the big picture, but this particular decade—2005 to 2015— had brought enough changes to make it feel like three. Back in 2005, most polling showed less than a quarter of women identifying as feminists. Hence that familiar refrain "I'm not a feminist, but ____."

By 2015, feminism, at least the word "feminism," was a mass-market brand. Ever since Beyoncé stepped out in front of that giant lit-up "FEMINIST" sign at the MTV Video Music Awards in 2014, the word—along with its partner word, badass—had become ubiquitous.

Badass feminism had broken off into tributaries like #KillAllMen and internet-driven "awareness campaigns" around societal afflictions like catcalling women on the streets. There was, of course, the perennial topic of office thermostats being set too low for women. "Air conditioning is another big, sexist plot" declared a much-discussed *Washington Post* article in 2015 with funny-not-funny impudence. The best way to be fashion-forward, it seemed, was to declare men the enemy.

Here's the problem with that sort of sentiment: It may purport to diminish male power, but in my view it only bolsters it. It hands men power they simply don't have, or at least don't deserve. It follows the logic of "punching up" in comedy, which says that it's okay to make fun of someone as long as that person intrinsically holds more power than you. It's why it's culturally acceptable to skewer a celebrity or a politician or even a random rich person but not a normal private citizen. (I guess unless that citizen has a lot of Twitter followers.) But here's what I think: When women apply this logic to men, bathing in their tears and shooing off their every utterance as mansplaining, they actually achieve the opposite of what they intended. They effectively put those men on pedestals they might not have been on to begin with. They lift them up in order to knock them down. They literally hand men their own power. It's like doing a jujitsu move against yourself.

Of course, fourth-wave feminism is forever armed with countless examples of how men have power over women: physically, economically, legislatively (that one is changing, albeit slowly). What many of its adherents don't seem to see, however, are the countless ways that women frequently have power over men: in the use of sex as a tool for manipulation, in parenting dynamics, in the ability nowadays to shut down a conversation by citing male privilege and dramatically dropping the mic. What they seem unwilling to confront are the ways that power dynamics shift among all kinds of people all the time. For all their thinking about theories of intersectionality among oppressed groups, too many women seem to have difficulty understanding why a homeless man who whistles at a young woman as she's off to her fancy internship every morning is not exactly a foot soldier for the patriarchy.

Yes, it sucks to be a woman sometimes. Until very recently, it usually sucked a whole lot more often than just sometimes. But there have always been ways in which it can suck to be a man, too. It can suck to be a person walking the earth in your own sensitive, sunburned, sweating, sagging skin. As George Carlin said, "Men are from earth; women are from earth. Deal with it."

But we don't deal with it. That's because, in some circles, dealing with it implies accepting it, and accepting it means being complicit in structural misogyny and so on. And the funny thing about it is that in assigning men undue power by seeing sexist injustices where there aren't any, it's all too easy to overlook other, very real injustices. One night I was riding the subway home to upper Manhattan, the train rattling through the Upper West Side and Harlem toward the Bronx. It was probably around eleven thirty or close to midnight, that hour when New York City starts to burble with a kind of tired, tipsy energy that, depending on where you are in life, tells you it's either time to go to bed or time to move on to phase two of the evening. The subway car wasn't empty, but it was hardly full. Two young men, probably in their twenties, sat across from me talking animatedly about something related to the arts, maybe theater or classical music. A gaggle of drunk-seeming young women, probably also in their late teens or early twenties, sat across from me a little farther down. Their skirts were short and their makeup was streaked and they were laughing and talking in that several-decibels-too-loud way that young women can be particularly good at. Something about their level of enthusiasm suggested they were not from the city but perhaps tourists or, more likely, suburbanites in town for someone's birthday or bridal shower.

At one point a man who was clearly intoxicated, mentally ill, or both (I'd bet my savings on both) got on the train and commenced with those flailing-around maneuvers that you often see in intoxicated, mentally ill people on the subway. He approached riders randomly, asking for money but also trying to engage them in conversation. When he got to me he began complimenting me, telling me I was pretty and remarking on my blonde hair. I did the thing I usually do with this sort of person, which is to acknowledge them in a good-humored sort of way to break the tension but not engage them any further. The man seemed angry that I wouldn't talk to him, so he set upon the group of girls, who, unlike me, seemed amused by him and invited him to sit down.

For several stops, the girls playfully teased the man, and he teased them back. I couldn't help but pick up on a certain voyeurism on their part. They were white and appeared to be middle class, and the man was black and probably homeless. I got the sense they were taking delight in what they perceived as his exoticism as well as pride in their willingness to let him sit with them. Other riders looked up from time to time, some rolling their eyes and some registering mild amusement. When the man finally got up to exit the train, he made a big show of telling the girls to have a great and beautiful night, and the girls, in turn, waved their arms and blew kisses at him.

I was sitting near the door, reading a magazine article

on my iPhone (an article about poverty and mental illness, coincidentally). As he passed me, the man stopped, leaned down right in my face, and shouted, "Now, *you* have a *fucked up* night!"

I raised both of my hands as if to surrender. "Okay, okay," I said. "I hear you."

"Bitch!" he shouted as he got off the train.

I was actually laughing a little. The phrase "have a fucked-up night" struck me as funny. The man had startled me, but not frightened me. I hadn't felt threatened at all. He was wiry and unsteady on his feet. If he'd attacked me, there were plenty of people around who could have—and surely would have—come to my rescue.

The young men directly across from me sat there looking horrified.

"I am so sorry," one of them said.

When I lived in New York decades earlier, when this sort of thing happened all the time, the passengers would have just shaken their heads and immediately forgotten about it. These men, however, were visibly upset.

"I'm just so sorry you had to go through that," the other one said.

"Well, what are you gonna do?" I said, turning back to my iPhone article.

"No, I'm really sorry," he said again.

"It's just so wrong," said the other man.

I realized then that this wasn't a display of concern but of self-flagellation. I looked at the men again. They had scruffy beards, longish hair, palish complexions. They spoke with that finely articulated cadence you often hear in people in the performing arts, especially theater people. I knew nothing about them, of course (they could have been computer programmers, for all I knew), but a quick flash of my imagination projected onto them recent liberal arts degrees with the full complement of intersectional doctrine. Despite looking like the kind of guys who might have been picked on in high school, they had grown into men who believed themselves to be oppressors. They had grown into men whose response to a mentally ill homeless guy calling a woman a bitch and telling her to have a fucked-up night was to apologize on behalf of the entire patriarchy.

But it wasn't the patriarchy that had yelled in my face. It was the mental health system, the homelessness problem, the drug war, the whole wounded city and wounded world. This wasn't systemic misogyny. It was life in the big city. Except life in the city has changed dramatically since I was the age of these young men. New York wasn't as rough in the 1990s as it was in the 1980s and 1970s. But even twenty-five years ago, that subway car could easily have been near empty at that time of night, especially as it passed Columbia University and approached Harlem. There could have been a mentally ill homeless guy in just about every subway car at all times. There would likely be people in that car with knives or guns or high on crack. The idea that giggling white girls from the suburbs would have been there at all, let alone invited a panhandler to sit down with them, was unthinkable.

The men went back to their conversation. They seemed a little baffled, maybe even disappointed, by my nonchalance. There had been so many things in play in that moment the man yelled in my face: class, race, gender, the changing economy of the city, the naïve hubris of a certain kind of white suburban girl, the low spark of smugness you see in a certain kind of aging person (this would be me) who clings to their toughness because they've lost hold of their youth. All of these things pushed and pulled against each other in a great mass of friction. The encounter played out on multiple planes. Yet it had been reduced to misogyny. It had been reduced to misogyny because those two scruffy-faced men had been educated about sexism in a way that handed them power that they didn't have. They then used that supposed power to apologize for something they didn't do. In the process, they literally—and quite inadvertently—patronized me. *How funny*, I thought. *How unfortunate.*

CHAPTER 4

You Are Lucky She's Cool:
Toughness, Toxicity, and the
Fall of the Fall of Man

I n 1996, in the same era I was having dinners with the older man in a powerful position, and my roommate and I were holding auditions for third roommates, the novel *Primary Colors* was published. It was a roman à clef about the Democratic primary race of a presidential candidate named Jack Stanton, an extremely thinly veiled Bill Clinton. Writing under the byline "Anonymous," the author was later revealed to be the political journalist Joe Klein.

Primary Colors was a huge best seller. Just as I'd listened to *Jagged Little Pill* in 1995 along with everyone else, in 1996 I read *Primary Colors* along with everyone else. Bill Clinton at the time was campaigning for his second term. It was the year he signed the welfare reform act into law, the year Jon-Benét Ramsey was murdered, the year the Yankees won the

World Series for the first time in nearly two decades. The death of Princess Diana was a year away, the discovery of the Bill Clinton–Monica Lewinsky affair two years away. The internet existed, but not really. I got my first e-mail account in 1996—AOL, naturally. Since there was hardly anything to do online, there was still plenty of time to read books.

I remember devouring *Primary Colors*. I do not remember thinking anything of the narrator being a black man even though the author was almost certainly a white man. Today this would be called out as an unforgivable act of racial appropriation (Michael Lewis's review in the *New York Times Book Review* merely pointed out that the narrator "is black when it serves the author's purpose but not when it doesn't"), but at the time it struck me as a clever way of eliding the fact that the narrator was really supposed to be Clinton operative George Stephanopoulos. Another character, Richard Jemmons, was supposed to be James Carville, the brilliant if also reptilian and degenerate strategist who would be largely credited with winning Clinton the election. The young women working as press assistants on the campaign are affectionately referred to in the novel as "press muffins." Richard, however, has taken to calling them all Winona thanks to his obsession with the actress Winona Ryder.

In an early scene, Richard approaches a press muffin at the copy machine and commences with some performative spasm of bravado before pulling out his penis.

Without flinching, the woman looks straight at it and says, "I've never seen one that . . . *old* before."

Richard is lacerated. He turns fuchsia. He "zips up and dashes out of there." There is applause in the office, and the woman curtsies.

"Man, you are lucky she's cool," the black George Stephanopoulos later says to Richard.

"I wouldna *done* it if she wasn't cool."

When I read this in 1996, I'm pretty sure I also thought the woman was cool. If the term "badass" had been in heavy rotation then, I probably would have thought she embodied that designation perfectly. Not that the stunt pulled in that scene was okay, but I remember thinking that if I ever had the misfortune of encountering such a situation at work, I'd hope I had the gumption to do something similar. Of course, I didn't know then what had happened to my friend Eileen just a year or so earlier in real life. It's also likely that in real life I probably wouldn't have the gumption to pull it off. It was a slick move in theory but an unlikely proposition in practice.

When I reread the novel a few years ago (a neighbor had left it on the freebie shelf in my building's laundry room, and I figured why not), I thought the scene was fine, but I was annoyed by the curtsy detail. It struck me as a man's fantasy of what a cool woman would do, just as the entire sensibility of the narrator was clearly a white person's fantasy of what a cool black person would be like. Cool would have been if the woman had just rolled her eyes and returned to her photocopying. The curtsy was totally uncool. In fact, it was worse than that. The curtsy was insulting. It was implying that the woman's coolness existed for the entertainment of others, that it was a performance begging for applause.

Reading on, another false note hit me in the face. Susan Stanton, the thinly veiled Hillary Clinton character (or Hillary Rodham character, as Clinton was then called), hands the thinly veiled James Carville's ass to him.

"Richard, you will not do that again . . . You will not even wink at a muffin. You will not call any person who works for us Winona, even if her name is Winona. If you do, the *best* you can hope for is that we'll can your butt. A more likely scenario is that I'll come after your scrawny little ding-a-ling with a pair of garden shears."

This is of course supposed to be loaded and symbolic and tragically prescient, since the thinly veiled Bill Clinton ends up getting caught sleeping with the hairdresser of the thinly veiled Hillary Clinton. But as a passage of dialogue it's prudish and corny and, from everything I've heard about Hillary Clinton, doesn't remotely capture how pissed she can get in the face of ill-behaving men. (In a later scene in *Primary Colors*, the Hillary character slaps the Bill character when she is presented with evidence of his cheating. Soap operatic as that is, it's also more like it.)

The scene at the copy machine may, in the span of a few short paragraphs, be as good a summation of the 1990s attitude around workplace gender relations as any of the myriad books written on the subject at the time. Here we have a young woman rising above the indignities of deplorable male behavior by cutting him down with a single word—"old"— delivered coyly and unflinchingly. There is no crying, getting angry, or calling the HR department.

There is no thought that, in twenty years' time, this woman formerly known as press muffin/Winona could conceivably go public about this moment, ending the career of this man who is not really James Carville with something like a single tweet. Instead, there is a constant ether of free-floating Darwinism. As on television series like *The West Wing* and, later, *Veep*, which clearly took certain tonal cues from *Primary Colors* even if they weren't specifically based on the book, you had the feeling the major job requirement for this workplace was stoicism. You had the feeling that everyone came to this workplace not just in spite of knowing they'd get roughed up a little but because they knew they'd get roughed up a little.

Again, the press muffin/Winona moment at the copy machine is a male writer's fantasy of how a young woman would respond to such an incident. It wouldn't surprise me if there was a whole genre of male heterosexual porn labeled "I wouldna *done* it if she wasn't cool." Still, for whatever reason (maybe the influence of 1980s movies like *Desperately Seeking Susan*, where Madonna's character might have made such a move), when I read it as a young woman, it was my fantasy as well. Today I would be told that such a reaction is nothing more or less than a steaming hot plate of internalized misogyny. I would be told that such a fantasy was just a spunkier version of fantasizing about becoming Don Draper's secretary and giggling while he pinches your ass all day. At the time, however, I was deeply invested in the idea of growing tougher with age.

My own first job out of college (not my beloved Film Society but a glossy magazine that was concerned primarily with skin exfoliation and that rudely awakened me to what it meant to have a real job) had been spiked with venomous personalities. The office was made up almost entirely of women and gay men, so sexual misconduct wasn't a major work hazard. Still, there was a spirit of hazing about the place, a kind of offhand abusiveness you tend to see in creative people who have been sentenced to day jobs putting out a commercial product.

My boss scared the hell out of me in the beginning, screaming at me for miswriting numbers on phone messages when in fact she'd misdialed the numbers, threatening to have me fired after I'd followed her orders to make reservations at one restaurant but she'd forgotten and showed up at another (the humiliation of standing there at Orso with no table ready!). The term "gaslighting" wasn't really in use back then, but my boss was a power gaslighter. I was miserable and desperate to quit until one day something changed. I yelled back at her. I can't remember what our dispute was over, just that for some reason I was compelled to match her tone. I said something sarcastic, something like "Why don't you learn to dial a phone?"

I don't recommend anyone try this at home. As far as boss/employee dynamics go, this is the exception that would prove all the norms that say it's better not to yell at your boss. But suffice it to say that my sudden burst of insubordination put a smirk on my boss's face that was quite clearly a strenuous effort to hold back a genuine smile. She said something like, "You think you're quite clever, don't you?" There was something charming about her use of the word "clever"; it had a cartoon villain quality to it that momentarily made me feel like I worked someplace more interesting than a beauty magazine. I responded along the lines of "I'm too clever for this job." It turned out my boss related to this sentiment deeply. She, also, was too clever for her job. From there, and in a perverse way, she became one of the best mentors I ever had. We continued to yell at each other for as long as I worked there. She continued to blame me when she showed up at the wrong restaurants. But something else happened, too. As soon as she figured out I had fledgling but promising editorial skills, she essentially let me do half her job while she spent much of the day at lunch. I came out of there, oddly enough, with skin that was at once better exfoliated and thicker than when I went in.

The rap on Gen Xers was always that we were politically apathetic, professionally unambitious, and cynical about relationships, family life, and the state of the world in general. There is truth to that, just as there is truth to the idea that we were—and perhaps still are—infused with irony, allergic to sentimentality, and committed to our detachment in ways that are fundamentally self-defeating. We were wary of the naïve utopianism of the 1960s generation, yet also frustrated that we never really had anything on offer to replace it. Even the *Time* cover story that announced our demographic existence in 1990 placed us firmly under the thumb of the baby boomers. The headline went: *Twentysomething: Laid back? Late blooming or just lost? America's next generation has a hard act to follow.*

The rap was that the Gen X identity was built around indifference. The iconic pop cultural images of our cohort—the *Breakfast Club* kids hanging out in detention, Ethan Hawke and Winona Ryder looking sexily bedraggled in *Reality Bites*— featured a lot of smirks, defiantly crossed arms, and expressions that fall somewhere between blank and fuck you. The idea was that the divorced parents and latchkeys around our necks and constant threat of nuclear annihilation had left us emotionally dampened. Before the age of "don't give a fuck," we were kicking it old school by not giving a shit.

I think that misses the mark. Our identities weren't built around indifference. They were built around toughness. Or at least the simulation of toughness.

Even as small children, there was nothing cooler than having a cast on your arm. As we grew up, the toughness landscape broadened to include emotional toughness. It was obvious, by age eight or nine, that resilience was where it was at. There was no greater gift of temperament than being able to laugh something off. There was no greater indignity than needing adult assistance or supervision. If both parents worked and we came home to an empty house, that could be as much a point of pride as of anxiety. We hated to be driven around by our parents, seen with them in restaurants, enabled by them in any way. We would no sooner tell our parents we were having sex than tell them we'd shoplifted half the inventory of Spencer Gifts. We got our driver's licenses the day we turned old enough. When we moved into our freshmen dorms at college, everyone knew that the coolest kids were the ones who'd made the trip by themselves.

As we got older, the toughness instinct built up in us like muscle mass. When we got dumped by romantic partners, Job One was to keep it together and not cry until we were safely alone. When we got harassed at work, we would no sooner call human resources than call our parents. When we got mugged on the subway, we'd be terrified and shaken. But we'd also know that this was part of the cost of doing business. This was an occupational hazard of occupying a territory larger and wilder than the one we probably had grown up in. (Unless we had grown up in big cities in the 1970s and '80s, in which case we one-upped our suburban friends by bragging about how we routinely got mugged on the way to school.) And we didn't even have to live in a big city to know what that meant. For us—for many of us—adulthood was analogous to a big city we had dreamt of moving to. We showed up hoping it would all work out. But like the press muffins in *Primary Colors*, we also showed up expecting to get tossed around a bit. That was, in some ways, part of the excitement.

This brings me (is it possible that it's taken me this many pages to get here?) to the curious, spurious, all-around horrendous case of Brett Kavanaugh and his road to the Supreme Court of the United States. If the fall of 2017 was the Fall of the Fall of Man, the fall of 2018 was, to borrow from Gabriel

García Márquez, the Autumn of the Patriarch. But unlike the deceased dictator in Marquez's 1975 novel, whose story is told in discursive, sometimes impenetrable flashbacks, the patriarchs of this season were both many in number and very much alive.

In the early weeks of October of 2018, women wearing *Handmaid's Tale* costumes gathered outside the Supreme Court holding signs that read "We the People Do Not Consent" and "Believe Survivors." Women on my social media feeds talked about how they couldn't sleep at night, how they couldn't stop crying during the day, how they didn't know how they could raise daughters in a country as violently woman-hating as this one. They exchanged tips on primal-scream techniques and other forms of self-care during this time of national crisis: aromatherapy, massage, driving to the recycling lot and hurling empty glass bottles into the bins with the force of Serena Williams's tennis serve. They fulminated about the toxic, clueless, antediluvian uselessness of men. They called for these men—white men, namely—to step back and be quiet for a year or two or ten and let women run things for a change. They issued the usual dictums about how the world would be a better place if women were in charge.

The occasion for this was not just Kavanaugh's conservative judicial record, but also—and overwhelmingly—the statements of Christine Blasey Ford, the woman brought forth by Senate Democrats to testify about Kavanaugh sexually assaulting her thirty-six years earlier, when they were in high school.

As Ford told it, she and Kavanaugh were among a small group of teenagers partying at a suburban Maryland house sometime during the summer of 1982 (being 1982 and all, there was no adult supervision at this party). In Ford's memory, she went upstairs to use the bathroom and two boys pushed her into a bedroom, wherein one of them jumped on top of her, grinded his body against hers, and clamped his hand down on her mouth to keep her from making any noise. Asked how certain she was that this boy was Brett Kavanaugh, Ford said, "I am one hundred percent certain."

I believed Ford and still do. That's not the same thing as knowing for sure what happened in that room all those decades ago. But having sat through just about every minute of the two-day proceedings I came away pretty much subscribing to the theory that things went pretty much as Ford described. I also believed, based on nothing more than my own conjecture, that Kavanaugh was blackout drunk and had no memory of it. Moreover, even though there was no one to corroborate Ford's account, there was still plenty of evidence that Kavanaugh was lying under oath about his history of excessive drinking. If that did not disqualify him from the job, not to mention his emotionally unhinged tirade following Ford's testimony (he sobbed and blamed the accusations on the Clintons), apparently nothing would. In the end, nothing did.

More germane to this discussion, though, is the way the entire saga became a twisted, tortured parable of the #MeToo movement and of identity politics in general. Both sides of the political aisle used the occasion to win points among constituents who hate the other side. Republican senator Lindsey Graham invoked the language of the white man silenced and aggrieved by the woke mob: "I know I'm a white man from South Carolina and I'm told I should shut up, but I will not shut up." Meanwhile, the moment Ford raised her right hand to be sworn in, the media turned her from a human being into a cultural and political symbol.

Though I found Ford's statements against Kavanaugh moving, compelling, and entirely credible, I was less moved by the sloganeering that rose up around them. Something about it felt hollow and perfunctory, as if Ford had become a meme before she even left the stand. Within hours of Ford's appearance at the Senate hearing, the mantra and meme #BelieveWomen was appearing on T-shirts and projected onto the sides of buildings. Democratic senators like Kamala Harris and Cory Booker were grandstanding to win points with their liberal voters. Harris called Ford a "true patriot." Booker, who'd made a show of bringing Ford a cup of coffee when she requested some caffeine, said, "How we deal with survivors who come forward right now is unacceptable. And the way we deal with this, unfortunately, allows for the continued darkness of this culture to exist."

Booker was correct in saying that the way we deal with survivors who come forward is unacceptable. That is because many of them, including Ford, didn't intend to come forward publicly. They were pushed into the spotlight by forces that, at least in this case, remain nebulous. I have no idea what sequence of events or what sort of political maneuvering led to

Democratic senator Dianne Feinstein holding on to Ford's allegations for months after Ford brought them to her. Nor do I know exactly how other accusers, like Julie Swetnick and Debbie Ramirez, came into the mix shortly after word got out that Ford was set to come forward. I do know that the timing did Blasey Ford and the Democrats no favors. It did little more than muddy the already turbid waters. And that is unacceptable given the hell that so many people, Ford and Kavanaugh most of all, were put through.

Swetnick's story was a weak goulash of memories of drunken parties wherein high school boys who may or may not have included Brett Kavanaugh deliberately incapacitated girls with drugs and alcohol in order to gang rape them. It was also, notably, brought to public attention by lawyer Michael Avenatti, who represented adult film actress Stormy Daniels in the case involving President Trump and who, of course, would later be arrested on federal embezzling and extortion charges, which he denied. Ramirez's story, first reported in the *New Yorker* by Ronan Farrow and Jane Mayer, was stronger, but at times left me with the impression that she was struggling to put a puzzle together more neatly than it could realistically be assembled.

"She was at first hesitant to speak publicly," Farrow and Mayer wrote in the *New Yorker*, "partly because her memories contained gaps because she had been drinking at the time of the alleged incident. In her initial conversations with the *New Yorker*, she was reluctant to characterize Kavanaugh's role in the alleged incident with certainty. After six days of carefully

assessing her memories and consulting with her attorney, Ramirez said that she felt confident enough of her recollections to say that she remembers Kavanaugh had exposed himself at a drunken dormitory party, thrust his penis in her face, and caused her to touch it without her consent as she pushed him away."

Let's go back to *Primary Colors* for a minute, specifically the scene where James Carville—I mean Richard Jemmons—exposes his penis to the press muffin at the copy machine. In the era in which this was supposed to have taken place, the early 1990s, this type of incident would have occupied a space somewhere between gross gag, stupid prank, and genuine violation. Now rewind to some ten years before that, in the early 1980s. Imagine a bunch of very drunk students at a prestigious Ivy League university horsing around at a party. Imagine that a male student exposed his penis to a female student in a very similar manner. Instead of this happening in front of an audience of spellbound colleagues working on a political campaign, imagine it happened among people likely too drunk to really register it at the time, let alone remember it later. Does this sound like a big deal?

I believe Ramirez's account of what happened at the party. Or at least I have no reason not to believe her. Again, this is not the same as *knowing* that it happened; as with Ford's description of her encounter with Kavanaugh, which I also believe, there is no way that anyone who wasn't there can know. The thing is, I have a hard time placing it into the category of "big deal." And until Kavanaugh was a Supreme Court nom-

inee, I wonder how Ramirez herself was categorizing it. "It was kind of a joke," Ramirez said in the *New Yorker*. "And now it's clear to me that it wasn't a joke." That is not to say she wasn't adversely affected by the incident. "I wasn't going to touch a penis until I was married," she told the *New Yorker*. "I was embarrassed and ashamed and humiliated."

But who, or what, exactly, made that clear? Ramirez's former classmates from Yale? Farrow and Mayer? The #MeToo movement itself? According to reports about the article, including a *Today* interview with Jane Mayer, e-mails about the incident had begun circulating between Ramirez and her Yale classmates in July. "Eventually, word of it spread," Mayer told *Today*'s Savannah Guthrie. "It spread to the Senate. It spread to the media. And we at the *New Yorker*, Ronan Farrow, my partner and coauthor on the story, reached out to her and she decided, after giving it really careful consideration for six days, she decided to talk to us about it."

Less than a week later, Ford took the stand and described, with far greater assurance, Kavanaugh holding her down on a bed and grinding against her while his buddy looked on. She said she was afraid he was accidentally going to kill her. She also mentioned the two boys laughing at her.

"Indelible in the hippocampus is the laughter," Ford said. "The uproarious laughter between the two and having fun at my expense. . . . I was underneath one of them while the two laughed. Two friends having a really good time with one another."

Sometimes I think it was this detail—the laughter—that

hit so many people in their souls. Unlike Anita Hill's testimony against Clarence Thomas twenty-seven years earlier, Ford managed to elicit the sympathy, even the empathy, of many men as well as women. Even if they couldn't bring themselves to believe it was Kavanaugh who assaulted her, they believed she was assaulted. They seemed to feel her pain. Maybe because if there's anything men know about humiliation, it's that it often comes in the form of ridicule by women. The famous Margaret Atwood quote that goes something along the lines of "Men are afraid that women will laugh at them, while women are afraid men will kill them" is overused, reductive, and not quite anything that Atwood actually ever said (in fact it was made famous when it showed up, in slightly different wording, in Gavin de Becker's best-selling book about female self-protection, *The Gift of Fear*), but it's not untrue. To fear for your life while also being laughed at by your peers is a particular sort of trauma, one that combines the worst of middle school with the worst of actual warfare.

But what an opera this has all become. What a Greek tragedy masquerading as a news cycle. In the Autumn of the Patriarch, as the balmy remnants of an Indian summer petered out with the last weeks of October, I felt like I was wedged into a narrow theater seat, desperate to go home despite barely having made it through the first act of the play. By Thanksgiving, slogans like #BelieveWomen, #BelieveSurvivors, and #BelieveHer had become their own subjects of controversy, with many conservatives and even some liberal types pointing out that their message fundamentally flew in the face of "innocent until proven guilty." Besides, the previous summer had seen two relatively high-profile examples of women being accused of sexual misconduct and even statutory rape, though both cases were so full of ironies and complications that they were almost too cumbersome to talk about. One was the case of Asia Argento, the Italian actress who was among the first to publicly accuse Harvey Weinstein of sexual assault and emerged as a leader in the #MeToo movement. In August of 2018, reports emerged, all of which Argento denied, that she paid off a young man who had accused her of sexually assaulting him years earlier, when he was seventeen and she was thirty-seven. Another case involved Avital Ronell, an eccentric and mercurial professor of German and comparative literature at New York University who was the subject of a Title IX investigation when a former graduate student named Nimrod Reitman accused her of sexually harassing him in a way that, according to the lawsuit, "asserted complete domination and control over his life."

In a display of irony that will be further underscored in the next chapter of this book, several feminist colleagues rushed to Ronell's defense, decrying the lack of due process. "We deplore the damage that this legal proceeding causes her, and seek to register in clear terms our objection to any judgment against her," they wrote in a letter to the university. "We hold that the allegations against her do not constitute actual evidence, but rather support the view that malicious intention has animated and sustained this legal nightmare."

I sat back and watched—or rather read about—this whole

saga as though it were a delicious prime-time soap opera, perhaps one entitled *As the Schadenfreude Turns*. Ronell, according to Reitman, had invited him to join her in Paris, where, he says, she pressed herself against him and kissed him repeatedly. And when Ronell lost electrical power during Hurricane Sandy in 2012, he said, she repeatedly showed up at his apartment and demanded to sleep there. Reitman alleged that Ronell's behavior over the course of his academic career amounted to "sexual harassment, sexual assault, and stalking."

Ronell denied all the charges, characterizing some of her affectionate language in e-mails as merely playful and "gay coded." This interpretation was backed up by an NYU colleague of Ronell's named Lisa Duggan, who said in a blog post that she had been "collecting cases of queer faculty accused of sexual harassment" and believed that "queers are disproportionately charged, often by homophobic or sexually confused students, sometimes by queer students whose demands for 'special' treatment are disappointed." The e-mails between Ronell and Reitman, Duggan said, were of a nature that "resonates with many queer academics, whose practices of queer intimacy are often baffling to outsiders."

The simple end to this story is that Ronell was suspended without pay for the 2018–19 academic year. The more accurate, and far more complex, set of conclusions to be drawn here may be less satisfying. That is to say that academia, especially the highly specialized and esoteric corners of the humanities in which this drama played out, is a labyrinth of egos, jealous gatekeeping, and the challenges of dealing with people whose outsize intellects are sometimes paired with quirky or possibly underdeveloped social skills. So confusing and specialized and "baffling to outsiders" is this labyrinth that when it comes to normal standards of human conduct, there is a sense that all bets are off. There is far more to the story, which isn't really worth going into here but which Masha Gessen outlined in an excellent August 25, 2018, *New Yorker* article about the whole affair. The morass of confusion and finger-pointing, Gessen said, amounted to "academics doing their job: engaging with things in great complexity. Discussions of #MeToo cases in other areas haven't been up to this task. We certainly can't expect it from Hollywood, whose job is to make stories palatable and simple. Writers, who on the subject of #MeToo have often practiced either avoidance or positional warfare, have been able to advance the conversation only so far."

That was the understatement of the year, or at least the understatement of the Autumn of the Patriarch. As that season trundled along, the Kavanaugh debacle moved the term "toxic masculinity" out of the ethos of Woke Twitter and into the mainstream embrace of the corporate wokescenti.

Like intersectionality, which I'll talk about in more detail a bit later, toxic masculinity is one of those concepts that, on its surface, makes perfect sense. It concerns the ways in which boys are raised to suppress their emotions and, in some cases, associate physical violence with power. But as tends to happen when trendy words like "toxic" are thrown in front of other words ("toxic person," "toxic relationship," "toxic workplace"), the whole concept has been diluted into zero-

calorie nothingness. Sure, there are stereotypically male behaviors that range anywhere from the merely unfortunate,
like not being able to share feelings with male friends, to the
truly terrible, like engaging in unnecessary physical violence
(and surely 99 percent of physical violence is unnecessary).

But what about all the stereotypically female behaviors
that can be equally toxic? What about the way women get
together and conduct withering assessments of other women
behind their backs—and then turn around and continue to
act like their best friends? What about the almost unfath-
omable level of cruelty that teenage girls can inflict upon one
another as they enforce social boundaries by shunning outsiders, both online and in real life? What about data (from
various sources, including the Centers for Disease Control)
that suggests rates of intimate partner violence among lesbian couples is just as high if not higher than rates among
heterosexual couples? Most women's social and emotional
manipulation skills are far more sophisticated than those of
most men, at least in my unscientific but anecdotally unassailable opinion. So isn't it a little unfair that men are getting
all the credit for being toxic?

And this is to say nothing of the manipulations and abuses
women can commit against men. Honestly, sometimes I wish
I could gather up all the women I've ever known, or encountered, and conduct this informal poll:

*Raise your hand if you've ever behaved badly and blamed it on
your period.*

Raise your hand if you've ever acted helpless in the face of an unpleasant-if-not-physically-demanding task like dealing with a wild animal that's gotten inside the house.

Raise your hand if you've ever coerced a man into sex even though he didn't seem to really want it.

Raise your hand if you've thought you were at liberty to do this coercing because men "always want it" and should feel lucky any time they get it.

Raise your hand if you've ever threatened to harm yourself if a man breaks up with you or doesn't want to see you anymore.

Raise your hand if you've been physically abusive with a male partner, knowing you'd be unlikely to face any legal consequences.

Raise your hand if you've lied about being on birth control, or faked a pregnancy scare, to see how a man would respond.

Raise your hand if you've ever manipulated a divorce or child custody dispute in your favor by falsely insinuating that a man has been abusive toward you or your child.

In this hypothetical gathering of every woman I've ever known or encountered (I'm imagining a football stadium at decent capacity), I'm certain there is not a single one of these questions that, if answered honestly, wouldn't send at least a few (in some cases many) hands into the air. Including my own. I'm guilty on the pest-control front. I also once tried to excuse an excessive display of irritability by saying I had PMS, which was a lie because it wasn't anywhere near that time of month (the truth is I'm just irritable a lot of the time). Don't get me wrong, I'm not saying lots of women do these things routinely. Most women, like most men, try to be decent people most of the time. What I am saying is that enough women do these things often enough that it's hypocritical, not to mention sexist, to constantly be on patrol for toxic masculinity when toxic femininity exists as well.

There are minor forms of feminine toxins, like blaming irrational temper tantrums on "being hormonal" or feigning helplessness to get what you want. And there are major toxins, many having to do with weaponizing your fragility so that those to whom you cause harm have a difficult time defending themselves, lest they look like the aggressors. Women, of course, can unleash these tactics on other women, be they romantic partners or not. But for the sake of this discussion, let's say we are talking about women and men and sex. We've established that many men are socially conditioned to think that women owe them sex. But what about the women who assume that men should be grateful for any sex they get?

Throughout my life, I've heard dozens of men tell stories about going ahead with sex even though they didn't really want to. I wasn't surprised to learn of a 2014 study, published in the journal *Psychology of Men & Masculinities*, that found that 43 percent of males in high school and college "reported they had an unwanted sexual experience and, of those, 95 percent said a female acquaintance was the aggressor." As the men I've talked to have put it, sometimes they went ahead with sex because they didn't want to hurt the woman's feelings. Other times, it was because they feared being perceived as having a low sex drive or as not being sexually interested in women. (Not without reason; in my younger years, it was not uncommon for a woman to console her female friend with "He must be gay!"

when the friend lamented a man's lack of interest in her. It was almost a corollary to "You *so* do not look fat in those pants!") A remarkable number of men have told me about times when women approached them and, often wordlessly, initiated sexual encounters without the slightest provocation or questions asked. I've heard, more than once, about unsolicited hand jobs on school buses when they were boys. Also, more than once, men have told me about past grade-school camping trips or overnight parties wherein girls they barely knew slipped into their sleeping bags or beds. In some cases, the men were happy to oblige the women's desires. In other cases, though, they went through with the encounters because they didn't want to make an awkward situation even more awkward.

These stories have been relayed to me in a tone I can only describe as bafflement. The men are not complaining, but nor are they boasting. If anything, they seem to be struggling to find the words to describe a not entirely welcome encounter that they felt they had no right to regard with anything other than gratitude. Needless to say, if you imagined any of these situations with the genders reversed, you'd have the potential for very different framing.

I realize that the physical size difference between most women and most men means that the comparison above isn't entirely fair; a woman who's sexually aggressive with a man is probably not putting him in insurmountable physical danger. And (obviously) for every bad behavior I mentioned in my list of questions there is an equal, opposite, and potentially more physically threatening form of bad behavior that men can, and do, visit upon women with just as much frequency. But that, right there, is precisely my point. In a free society, everyone, regardless of gender, or any other identification, is free to be a manipulative, narcissistic, emotionally destructive asshole.

I'll say it again: I believed Christine Blasey Ford's testimony about what happened between her and Kavanaugh when they were in high school. But this is my personal belief, based on nothing more than gut feeling, that things transpired more or less as Ford described them and that Kavanaugh was too drunk at the time to remember. There is a difference between believing and knowing. All the truth digging in the world will not change the fact that all kinds of people misrepresent, misremember, misinterpret, and willfully or unwillfully make misleading statements for all kinds of reasons. In fact, Mark Judge, whom Ford said was in the room, told the FBI that he did not recall the party and denied witnessing the alleged assault.

My list of "raise your hand" questions will surely set some teeth on edge. It's difficult to talk about things like women tricking men into getting them pregnant, not least of all because it makes you sound like a part of the men's rights movement—a loosely knit and often self-defeating enterprise that overrides legitimate grievances (about, say, the family court system) with ambient misogyny and conspiracy theories. It can also be a slippery slope to appearing overly sympathetic with so-called incels, a similarly incoherent, self-defeating, and occasionally dangerous subculture of men who hate women because they can't find any who will have sex with them.

But the thing about growing older is that, as time goes on,

you run into more and more people. That means you bear witness to the different forms of havoc human beings can wreak. When I was in my twenties, just hearing a phrase like "tricking men" would have made me assume it was coming from a woman-hating kook. The phrase does sound antiquated, after all. But by now, I've seen all kinds of people attempt all manner of tricks, sometimes for their own amusement and sometimes because they're legitimately disturbed. I know men who, amid contentious divorce proceedings, have been accused, preposterously, of spousal and child abuse. I know women who are so skilled in the dark art of gaslighting that the targets of their mind games, be they boyfriends or BFFs, don't stand a chance. Once, while working with high school students, I overheard some girls joking to one another about how they were going to go out that night and "hit on older guys who don't know we're underage and later be, like, 'Dude, you're a pedophile.'"

I decided to give the girls the benefit of the doubt and assume they were just goofing around, condemning misogynist stereotypes about young women as jailbait by ironically reclaiming those stereotypes. Along the way, I tried to think like a good feminist and consider that patriarchal societies foster or even force this kind of manipulative female behavior because it's often the only power available to women. But that's an excuse and a poor one. Some women act abominably because some people act abominably. Both sexes contain multitudes.

We are all, as George Carlin suggested, incorrigible, insufferable, equally defective earthlings. Deal with it.

CHAPTER 5

....

What Hath One Lecture Wrought!: Trouble on Campus

Nearly thirty years ago, when I was a sophomore at Vassar College in Poughkeepsie, New York, student activists made national headlines when they seized control of the college's main administration building and disrupted campus life for several days. The inciting incident was an offhand comment made by New York senator Daniel Patrick Moynihan, a legendary liberal and champion of women and minorities (that was the phrase back then, "women and minorities") who had come to campus to receive an honorary title called the Eleanor Roosevelt Chair. Moynihan gave a lecture in conjunction with the award and spoke with students, staff, and community members at a reception afterward. It was here that many witnessed him making a racist remark to a woman named Folami Gray. The remark was perceived by at least a few people, including Gray herself, as racist.

This was well before the days of ubiquitous recording devices; there's never been complete consensus on what was actually said and what was meant by it. Most reports, however, suggest that Gray, who directed a local youth organization and was of Jamaican descent, challenged a statement Moynihan had made about America being "a model of ethnic cooperation." At this, Moynihan is said to have told Gray something to the effect of "if you don't like it here, why don't you pack your bags and go back to where you came from?"

Moynihan then turned to a student, who, perhaps in an effort to diffuse the tension, asked if he was a senior senator. Gray interjected and said, "He's a senior racist!"

This was decades before the age of memes, but there's no telling what sort of viral load a phrase like "senior racist" could carry today. (You can imagine a GIF of Betty White shaking her finger in the spirit of "you're not calling me a senior racist!") Nor were we anywhere near the era of clickbait headlines like "Aging White Male Senator Insults Woman of Color at College Wine and Cheese Reception and *You Won't Believe What Happens Next!*"

Here's what did happen next. A group emerged that called itself the Coalition of Concerned Students. The coalition held a series of meetings over two weeks that included representatives from a variety of campus political and social organizations (the Black Students' Union and the Vassar Jewish Union, among them). There was no specific agenda initially. As one leader told the student newspaper, *The Miscellany News,* "We were trying to form a unity between student groups on campus to seek some solidarity. We thought that as a united group, we might be able to get a little more action out of the administration on concerns that each of the individual groups had been voicing to no avail for weeks, for months, for years."

Early in the morning of the first day of demonstrations, students began blocking doors to the college's administration building, a large multiuse building called "Main," which stands at the end of the campus's main driveway. They barred entrance to all but other protesters and those who lived in the building's dormitory area. The next day, hundreds of students had joined in the protest. Classes were canceled as people rallied outside Main, chanting, playing bongos, and, in my memory, holding up at least one empty chair in reference to "de-chairing Moynihan."

According to the *Miscellany News,* the protesters told the college president, Frances Ferguson, she had two days to respond to their demand that Moynihan be removed from the chair. (Moynihan, for his part, said he had no recollection of the incident with Gray, though he did correct the record and say he had not talked in his lecture about "a model of ethnic cooperation" but had said that "the United States of America provides a model of a reasonably successful multi-ethnic society.")

By this time, national news outlets were covering the controversy, including the *New York Times* and CNN. Moynihan finally relinquished the chair and returned the $1,000 that had come with it. The *New York Times* appeared to take some delight in relaying highlights from his letter to Ferguson:

"Heavens, what hath one lecture wrought! . . . I know you won't approve of this, and I'm sure Eleanor Roosevelt would not have done, but let me do so anyway. The times, unhappily, have changed . . . [I can] scarce believe the present ruckus . . . [and do] not want to prolong it."

The protesters, for their part, were happy to prolong the ruckus. They issued the president a list of further demands that hit upon a range of social justice issues, from divesting in South Africa to establishing a black student center to calls for total transparency about how tuition dollars are allocated. They also wanted a college rabbi, an intercultural center, and better wheelchair access throughout the campus.

By now, it might not come as a surprise to you that I thought the protests were mostly theater. As such, I mostly carried on about my business, which frankly was what most students did. (Like many campus protests today, it was a small but loud minority of students that led the revolt; most of us just wanted to go to class so as not to squander our tuition dollars.) I was dimly aware of the demands and thought they seemed not unreasonable, but mostly I was struck—even surprised—by the passion of the students. As with many urbane, East Coast enclaves of privilege, the social temperature of Vassar ran decidedly cool. It was important to seem smart, but even more so, it was important to not appear to get too excited or upset about anything. This wasn't so much about not caring, but about making clear that you recognized the limitations of caring even while in the process of caring. (This applied to everything from getting good grades to doing well in sports to getting a boyfriend or girlfriend, where the implicit idea was that if any of the above required strenuous effort, it was perhaps a sign that there were better ways you could be spending your time.)

It's not that I was indifferent to activism. A year earlier, I had joined dozens of my classmates as we boarded buses to Washington, D.C., to march in an abortion-rights rally organized by the National Organization for Women. There were an estimated 600,000 marchers that day, and I remember how good it felt to stand with my friends in our matching college sweatshirts shouting "Never again!" and "My body, my choice!"

For some reason I could not fully board the bus of the Moynihan protest. Maybe it was because the student protests seemed like such a departure from the coolness posture, but I couldn't get past the feeling they were at least partly performance art.

That's not to say those involved were consciously performing. On the contrary, they had genuine and long-standing gripes about how the school was run and had had the good strategic sense to seize this opportunity to get those gripes heard. I just couldn't shake the perception that they weren't protesting so much as doing impersonations of protesters. I felt guilty about feeling that way even at the time, and I'm still ashamed to admit it now, but that's where my head was. For some reason, I saw just about everything through the lens of artifice back then. The guy playing guitar in the dormitory stairwell wasn't reveling in the joy of music but Playing the Part of the Guy Who Played Guitar in the Stairwell. The people who returned from junior year abroad experiences in the Middle East wearing those black-and-white-checkered Palestinian scarfs known as kaffiyehs weren't interested in freeing Palestine, as they would be today, but rather just signaling that they'd been someplace exotic. In some cases, "exotic" meant the East Village in New York City, where you could buy kaffiyehs from street vendors, along with sunglasses and "I Love New York" kitchen magnets. I know because that's where I bought my kaffiyeh, which I wore with a vintage leather car coat in an effort to prove to myself that I wasn't just a bland girl from the suburbs. All this is to say that the reason I felt like everyone was impersonating a college student more than actually being one was because *I* was impersonating a college student more than actually being one.

Save my years for graduate school and then later as an instructor at Columbia (which, despite having a proper campus, has always felt to me like an extension of the city), I would not spend significant time on a traditional college campus again until the earliest days of the Trump era, when I would go to the University of Iowa for a teaching stint. January of 2017 was a strange time to arrive in a liberal university town in a red heartland state. But that is where I found myself, teaching nonfiction writing to graduate students in Iowa City.

This was a semester-long gig that I had accepted nearly a year earlier, a time that, once I arrived in Iowa, felt like another historical period altogether. Back in New York, as I'd prepared for my trip, the open wound of the November election made the 2016 holidays feel like a party no one was really in the mood to attend. Come Inauguration Day, we would all effectively report to prison for a minimum four-year sentence. Come the New Year, I would get in my car with my dog and drive to Iowa City. By then, any excitement I'd had about the job had given way to a hazy sense of foreboding. Teaching sensitive, young people was challenging even in non-apocalyptic times. This might all prove to be too much.

I drove through sleet and snow on Interstate 80 for two days until I arrived to a flat, frozen land that wouldn't thaw until just before my return in the spring. During my months in Iowa, I often felt like I was walking through fog so thick I could see little more than my hand in front of my face. The world—not just Iowa, but the whole world, at least the whole country—was a place utterly without perspective. There was no depth of field, no sense of context. Everyone seemed to be reacting to every piece of news like a toddler reacting to the needle stick of an immunization; so unprecedented was this particular pain sensation, so uncertain was the knowledge that it was ever going to end, that it could be met only by screams of terror. Everyone, no matter their station in life, was enraged, scared, confused, paranoid, despondent—at least if they were liberals, which can be said of most people in Iowa City. (The town, which has a population of around 75,000, went solidly for Hillary Clinton; the state itself favored Trump by almost ten percentage points.)

By the time I got to Iowa, I'd been observing the college political scene for a few years, both as an instructor and as a follower of endless news stories about the ideological warfare happening mostly on liberal arts campuses. In trying to distill my observations into written words, I always found myself in what ultimately amounted to an endless game of Whac-a-Mole. Every time I sat down to document the latest uprising at an institution of higher learning, the story would be eclipsed by a yet more egregious example of late-adolescent leftist sanctimony run amok. More frustratingly, every time I thought I'd seen the worst of it, I saw something better. By which I mean I saw something that suggested the situation was better than I'd thought it was. Or at least getting better. Or at least not becoming measurably worse. But then something ridiculous would happen all over again—like Harvard law students calling for a law professor and faculty dean to resign (and publicly apologize) in February 2019 because the professor had joined Harvey Weinstein's defense team and this was "trauma-inducing"—and I'd be back to where I started. (For what it's worth, in May, Harvard acquiesced somewhat to students and announced that the professor would leave his position as a faculty dean, though he would remain on the faculty.)

Maybe it's best put this way. When it comes to the American college campus, the climate is at once not nearly as bad as it's made out to be and far worse than you could ever believe. The "snowflake" reports we've seen for the last several years in the news and on social media—("Colleges Offering 'Safe Space' for Naps," "U. Kansas resident advisor warned against 'very masculine' gorilla image in jungle-themed decor")—have done a masterful job of cherry-picking the most egregious displays of collegiate radicalism, but they never tell the whole story. They tell the parts that are fun to laugh about. They tell the parts that can be boiled down to a 140-character tweet, a clickbait headline on Google News, an indignant post from your Facebook friend who didn't bother to get all or even most of the facts. No doubt you're familiar with the greatest hits of the last few years: the meltdowns over offensive Halloween costumes (or, really, just the *idea* of offensive Halloween costumes) at Yale, the Oberlin students who complained that the dining hall sushi was culturally insensitive, the academic journal that deemed Starbucks's pumpkin-spiced lattes a symbol of white privilege.

Aficionados of this genre of news might find themselves regular readers of digital sites like Campus Reform and Inside Higher Ed. Here they can choose from any number of varieties of the low-hanging fruit that have come to represent student activism and "PC culture." They can hear about intersectional theory and inclusion and privilege (this is not necessarily the same as learning or understanding what these things actually mean). They can learn just enough about trigger warnings and safe spaces to make them grouse about the aforementioned "special snowflakes" and the abject entitle- . ment and fragility of "all millennials" without realizing that the stories they keep hearing represent but a tiny fraction of an enormous generational cohort in American history.

The most recent Pew Research data shows that millennials, who are usually defined as those born between 1981 and 1996, are estimated to now number around 71 million (this is according to the latest census data for which population estimates are available). By contrast, there are now around 74 million baby boomers (at their peak population, in 1999, there were nearly 79 million of them) and a paltry 65.8 million Gen Xers (that's our peak, by the way). In 2017, some 20 million people could count themselves as college students, meaning they were enrolled in some kind of institution of higher learning.

The ones yelling and picketing and pulling fire alarms when someone with digressive views comes to speak on campus are actually but a fraction of those who fall under the rubric of "college student." Most students, by and large, are too busy studying and working multiple jobs and generally trying to pull themselves up the socioeconomic ladder to get involved in political or social activism. The "social justice warriors," or SJWs, we hear about on the news are a small but obstreperous minority.

Still, even at a place like the University of Iowa, a public institution whose 33,000 students lean toward football and fraternities more than gender theory and Marxism, there are clusters of leftist activism in just about every direction. One spring evening in late April of 2017, I sat on the grass outside the Old Capitol building on campus watching a Take Back the Night rally. Take Back the Night is a nonprofit organization and also a sort of umbrella term for a type of protest event where survivors of sexual assault and domestic abuse gather in solidarity and often publicly share their stories. I remember Take Back the Night rallies from my own college days; some of my friends had attended and said they were deeply affected by the experience. A few who were survivors of trauma said that the gatherings had given them the much-needed feeling that they weren't alone.

The crowd on the lawn at Iowa consisted of sixty or so students and a smattering of faculty, staff, and people from the community. When I arrived, a young woman in cargo pants and a hoodie was speaking into a microphone. She read from her phone, her thumb scrolling as quickly as she spoke.

Her words were powerful. Framed as a letter to a relative who had abused her, the words sounded almost like poetry. *Why did you touch me when I was seven, and again when I was twelve?*, the woman asked. *Why did you climb in my bed?* With rising emotion but without breaking down, she went on to describe a wrenching pattern of incest, denial, and, finally, the cognitive dissonance she felt when she cared for this relative as he lay dying in a hospital bed, never betraying her secret so as to protect other family members. *I let them remember you the way they wanted to. I didn't do that for you.*

Next up was a young man, presumably gay, who talked

about thinking "this kind of problem" didn't have anything to do with someone like him. "But then someone I thought was my friend took advantage of me." This speaker was followed by another man, presumably straight, who got up and delivered a monologue so filled with platitudes you'd think it had been compiled from public service announcements. *We are all victims of this society, but we are also the survivors that can transform the culture. We must end rape culture and move toward consent-driven culture.*

A woman stepped up to the mic and began describing a series of fumbling maneuvers under blankets with a male friend. Her story was opaque and glancing, like a dream you try to recollect in the morning. There were hands (his) and blood (hers). There was, by her description (and to my mind, though I'm not a doctor), more blood than would likely result from even the most aggressive digital deflowering. There was the added detail that "I didn't know it was rape" until weeks later.

Her emotion was contagious. Sadness for her welled in my throat. I may have wondered about the accuracy of some of the details in her story, but her feelings were impossible to wonder about. There was no question she was in pain. Something had hurt her and that hurt now encircled her.

I had recently met a young man—I'll call him Joseph—who had his life upended earlier that year when a woman reported him to the dean of students for sexual misconduct. It's not that I thought this woman could have been the one who reported Joseph. I was certain she was not. Still, aspects of her story reminded me of the one Joseph had relayed to me. With both this young woman and Joseph's accuser, there appeared to have been some lag time between the actual encounter and the conclusion that something criminal had occurred. (For Joseph's part, he'd thought the encounter, albeit awkward, was totally consensual.) I could imagine any number of avenues the woman could have taken to reach this conclusion. Maybe she really was so naïve as to what constituted rape that it took weeks to arrive at the answer to what for someone else might have been a very simple equation.

Or maybe the equation wasn't so simple. Maybe an activist-minded friend helped reframe the encounter from something awkward into something criminal. Maybe she stumbled upon a Tumblr account expounding on the qualities of rape-you-didn't-realize-was-rape and it proved revelatory. Maybe—and unlikely as it seemed, I'd heard enough about this sort of thing not to rule it out—the woman told her mother, or even both parents, about the encounter. And maybe those parents gave in to some kind of primal parental inclination to believe that their daughter had not gotten herself into an unpleasant sexual predicament of her own volition but was instead manhandled against her will like the gentle flower all parents know their daughters to be. And, maybe, to appease those parents, the young woman adopted that version of events for herself.

Or not. I could have been all wrong. Certainly none of my hypotheticals were entirely right. Most likely, the facts of the situation were buried beneath so many layers of interpretation and reinterpretation that trying to figure out the truth was beside the point. As the woman stood before the crowd, looking triumphant, it occurred to me that no matter what had happened to her, no matter how large that trauma figured in her memory and self-concept, the main event was perhaps taking place right now. However much blood there was or wasn't, it was this new state of being, this deliverance into survivorship, that possibly was most important now.

I chewed over these thoughts as my pants became laced with grass stains. I remembered how George Will had entertained thoughts along the same lines in a *Washington Post* column in 2014 and was duly eviscerated not just on social media and in the feminist blogosphere but by the overall media establishment. Questioning the relentlessly repeated statistic about one in five women being the victims of sexual assault during college, Will (as I was reminded when I went home from the rally that evening and looked it up on the internet) characterized this victimhood as a "coveted status that confers privileges." He lamented the federal overreach that forces colleges and universities to enact chaotic adjudication procedures that leave the accused party with few due process rights. Predictably, Will was tarred as sexist, out of touch, and, naturally, a rape apologist.

For my part, I remember feeling like Will was essentially correct and yet incredibly stupid for mounting such an argument in something as public as a newspaper column. I was writing a newspaper opinion column myself then, and whenever I dipped my toe into the waters of campus sexual politics I made sure to burn major calories letting my readers know that I was aware sexual assault was really, *really* bad and should be taken really, *really* seriously and that expanding its definition into relative meaninglessness (some codes of conduct classify things like a grope at a crowded party as assault) denigrates victims more than it empowers them. I also noted that Will had made a classic columnist error and tried to cram about six different ideas into 750 words (pro tip: don't exceed one idea per 800 words). He went on about microagressions, speech codes, college drinking, the fungible nature of statistics, due process, and the Obama administration's ham-handed initiative to establish a rating system for universities.

As a result, his underlying point, which (at least by my reading) was that elevating victimhood actually minimizes the seriousness of assault, got bollixed up in thousands of misreadings and ideologically driven backlash. "It's Time to Fire George Will," rang the headline in *U.S. News & World Report*. "If *The Washington Post* does decide to fire Will, it will at least send a message that all women have the right to live free of sexual assault," wrote a columnist in *Psychology Today*. Scripps College disinvited Will from a speaking engagement. Four U.S. senators with "an ongoing interest in ways to reduce sexual assaults on college campuses" (their wording) wrote a letter to Will censuring him for trivializing what they called the "scourge" and "spreading epidemic" of campus rape. Media Matters, a progressive organization devoted to fighting misinformation in conservative media, later named Will "Misinformer of the Year."

Will refused to back down, saying in an open letter to the four senators published in the *Washington Post* that he believed he took sexual assault more seriously than his critics, "which is why I worry about definitions of that category of crime that might, by their breadth, tend to trivialize it."

As I sifted through the digital wake of this brouhaha, I found myself grappling with the same cognitive dissonance that follows me into just about every discussion about campus sexual assault. I've never been the victim of assault myself. I came damn near close once when a stranger followed me on a dark street—and no, I'm not talking about the ginger-haired guy who shoved my collarbone. But the number of women and men I know who are not so lucky could probably fill a medium-size sports arena, probably one with even greater capacity than my aforementioned football stadium filled with toxic females. Many of these assaults took place in childhood at the hands of family members or other known parties. In some cases, the abuse left a psychological imprint that somehow set victims up to be targets for further abuse throughout their lifetimes.

When it comes to the "one in five" statistic, it's important to know what's being measured and how. I'll talk more about that in a few pages, but for now I'll say I'm more inclined to give credence to data that suggests one in five girls is a victim of childhood sexual abuse. That comes from the National Center for Victims of Crime, which puts the rate of childhood sexual abuse of boys at around one in twenty (this sounds low to me, actually). There's also data showing that people who suffer sexual trauma as children are more likely to be revictimized as adults, including almost fourteen times more likely to be assaulted in college, according to the U.S. Department of Health and Human Services. A friend who'd survived such trauma once put it this way: "After you're abused once, you become a target. It's almost like they can smell it on you."

I'll return to Joseph. He told me he'd been a virgin when he came to college. He'd had a few girlfriends in high school, he said, ones he'd met through his Catholic youth activities, but it was all fairly chaste. Early in his first semester at the University of Iowa, Joseph heard through friends that a girl in one of his classes liked him. That is to say, her friends told his friends that she thought he was cute. Joseph received this news favorably. As such, a date was arranged, at least insofar as any college student, in my time or in these times, ever goes on a date. That is to say they hung out.

They hit it off, he told me. The date lasted many hours and included stopping by a house party off campus and later swinging by a burger place. Joseph said the woman kept talking about a movie she loved that he'd never seen, and they decided to go back to his dorm room to watch it. It was by now around two a.m., and Joseph's roommate was asleep in the bottom bunk bed, but they climbed into the top bunk and began watching the movie on his laptop.

"She kept looking away from the movie and looking up at me," Joseph recalled. "Like craning her neck like she wanted something."

He said he was happy just to watch the movie. He liked this girl and didn't want to rush anything. Besides, he was tired and his roommate was asleep right below them. But then she abruptly stopped the movie.

"She slapped the laptop closed and said, 'You don't get it, do you?'" Joseph told me. "And she just kind of climbed on top of me and started making out."

What Joseph described next I'll relay here to the best of my ability, and depending on your inclination, you can mentally underscore it with a bass line from the grumbling chorus or not. He said the woman seemed eager to have sex and that he told her he'd never done it before and asked if she was sure she wanted to. When she said that she did want to have sex, he got out a condom but lost his erection as soon as he put it on. Some time later (and here the details are fuzzy and admittedly I didn't want to pry) they managed to have intercourse but without the condom. Even so, he says, the woman gave no indication of regretting what had happened, though she did turn down his offer to walk her back to her dorm.

A few days later, Joseph told me, the woman texted him and said that she was worried about the unprotected sex and wanted him to send her money via a digital-wallet app so she could buy the Plan B birth control pill. He said he readily complied and that they had a few friendly or at least cordial

exchanges after that. Two weeks later he received a letter from the dean of students saying that he was being brought up on unspecified sexual misconduct charges. Afraid to tell his parents, he consulted a lawyer, whose fee he could never begin to afford. Still, he went to an initial meeting with the associate dean of students, feeling not terribly worried, since he was confident that he hadn't done anything wrong. The associate dean gave little hint as to how Joseph's story was going over, saying only, "It sounds like you came in here prepared."

A little background on what "prepared" might mean in this case, which I'm going to lay out in some detail because I believe that some of the people with the strongest opinions about this issue don't fully grasp just what they're opining about. It all started with the now-infamous mandate known as the "Dear Colleague Letter." In 2011, a wing of the U.S. Department of Education, called the Office for Civil Rights, sent a nineteen-page letter to more than 7,000 colleges and universities stating that their federal funding would be at risk if they were found not to be "taking immediate and effective steps to end sexual harassment and sexual violence." To make this directive legal, it was tucked under the rubric of Title IX, the 1972 education statute that prohibited discrimination in schools on the basis of sex. The idea was that victims of sexual assault or misconduct who were forced to remain in school with their assailants were being deprived of their rights under Title IX.

Foremost among the immediate and effective steps was the requirement that, when adjudicating sexual assault complaints, schools use a standard of proof known as the prepon-

derance of evidence. This meant that officers who heard a case could find a student guilty of misconduct even if those officers were only 51 percent convinced of the student's guilt. (In the actual judicial system, criminal cases like sexual assault are held to the higher standard of "beyond a reasonable doubt." The preponderance-of-evidence standard is used in civil cases.)

It was odd enough that the government was ordering campus tribunals to withhold due process rights in ways that would never be tolerated in the outside world. Worse in many ways, though, was that the other immediate and effective steps were subject to interpretation by individual colleges and universities. And because administrators were terrified of losing federal funding—in an off-the-record conversation in 2016, the dean of a prestigious liberal arts college told me he had essentially lived in a perpetual state of confusion, exasperation, and paranoia since 2011—most erred on the side of the most stringent implementation.

The inconsistency effectively resulted in a kangaroo-court system throughout American universities. There were cases of accused students being sanctioned without even being informed of the charges against them. There were cases where accusers were not permitted to be cross-examined while defendants were forced to answer questions without being informed of their rights or allowed to have an attorney present. Even more troubling, the inconsistency allowed universities to get away with playing fast and loose with the rules to protect certain parties. In other words, a star athlete accused of

assault could theoretically be subject to different proceedings than a regular guy on an academic scholarship.

So there's my attempt at a cursory overview of the effects of the Dear Colleague Letter. Others have dug into it with far more depth and context than I need to here. Emily Yoffe has done outstandingly thorough reporting in places like *Slate* and the *Atlantic*, as has Robby Soave in *Reason*. In her 2017 book *Unwanted Advances: Sexual Paranoia Comes to Campus*, the Northwestern University professor Laura Kipnis offered a meticulous and rather gobsmacking account of the ways in which Title IX can be a runaway train. But there's a reason I wanted at least to summarize it here. Many people reading this book who care about the problem of campus sexual assault automatically assume that whatever the Obama administration did to curb it was unequivocally the right thing to do. These are the people who were appalled in September 2017, when Betsy DeVos, the education secretary under President Trump, announced her intention to roll back the guidelines of the Dear Colleague Letter.

"The era of 'rule by letter' is over," DeVos said, adding that "any school that refuses to take seriously a student who reports sexual misconduct is one that discriminates. And any school that uses a biased system toward finding a student responsible for sexual misconduct also commits discrimination."

Never mind that all DeVos said was that the policy was going to be reviewed through a notice-and-comment period and that nothing was happening imminently. Never mind that

Harvard Law professor and *New Yorker* writer Jeannie Suk Gersen did the nearly unthinkable and gave DeVos the imprimatur of that publication, writing on the *New Yorker* website that "DeVos appears to be proceeding exactly as an agency head should . . ." The online indignati set the tone. "Breaking: @Betsy DeVosED just made campuses safer for rapists," said the Women's March Twitter account. A *Slate* headline went "Finally, a New Policy We Know Trump Truly Believes in: Protections for Sexual Assaulters." When DeVos met not just with survivor advocacy groups but also with groups like Families Advocating for Campus Equality (FACE) and Stop Abusive and Violent Environments (SAVE), which advocate for due process rights for accused men, she was likened to a men's rights activist. Joe Biden, eager for any opportunity to anneal his brand as an avuncular champion of women (sure, he mishandled the Anita Hill hearing back in 1991, but, hey, had he not introduced the Violence Against Women Act in 1990?), called the decision "shameful." The hashtag #StopBetsy picked up speed on Twitter, with activists like Amy Siskind tweeting that DeVos's proposal was "the next step on our path to authoritarianism."

I understand the sentiment and simmering—okay, boiling over—frustration. I may have been less apoplectic than many of my liberal friends in the face of this particular recommendation, but I'm still a liberal and still find DeVos to be a troubling, even repugnant, specimen. I think she has no business being in the position she is in. I recoil at just about every idea she puts forth. I believe her school voucher program is

Christian proselytizing in disguise. However, I also strongly suspect that if the rollback of the Dear Colleague Letter had come from a more palatable source, very few people would have blinked an eye. Because the truth is that the policy wasn't working. Plenty of liberals, even liberal feminists, had been saying so for a long time. As far back as 2014, twenty-eight professors at Harvard Law School published an open letter in the *Boston Globe* calling the Obama policy, which Harvard had just enacted, "overwhelmingly stacked against the accused" and "inconsistent with many of the most basic [due process] principles we teach." Three years later, just weeks before DeVos's announcement in 2017, four of those professors, Janet Halley, Elizabeth Bartholet, Nancy Gertner, and Jeannie Suk Gersen, all self-avowed feminists, sent a memo to the Education Department in support of DeVos's rollback, saying the definitions of sexual misconduct had been made far too broad. "They go way beyond accepted legal definitions of rape, sexual assault, and sexual harassment," they wrote. "The definitions often include mere speech about sexual matters. They therefore allow students who find class discussion of sexuality offensive to accuse instructors of sexual harassment."

A little over a year later, the Department of Education formally released its proposal. The policies were enough for the liberal apoplexia to reprise itself, but, upon inspection, not really enough to enact meaningful change. Schools would have the option of adopting higher evidentiary standards and cross-examining accusers, but not necessarily be compelled to. Still, the fact that the dictum was coming from DeVos made it resistant to reasoned reaction. "A woman appointed by a serial sexual abuser wants to make it harder to punish college sexual abusers," Jessica Valenti tweeted. Alyssa Milano made a video in which she compared DeVos to the Grinch and referred to the rollback as a "shIXtty gift" that everyone should take and shove it right up her . . . notice and comment section.

Democratic lawmakers, too, rushed in to signal their opposition on social media. Representative Maxine Waters of California tweeted "Betsy DeVos, you won't get away with what you are doing. We are organizing to put an end to your destruction of civil rights protections for students." Joe Biden wrote on Facebook that the proposal "would return us to the days when schools swept rape and assault under the rug and survivors were shamed into silence." The American Civil Liberties Union, apparently confused about its purported mission of protecting the constitutional rights of all citizens, unleashed a tweet thread denouncing the rollback because "it promotes an unfair process, inappropriately favoring the accused . . . We will continue to support survivors." They later issued an official statement that was more comprehensive and hewed (somewhat) closer to their mission. Nonetheless, to hear the ACLU talking about "inappropriately favoring the accused," even on a platform like Twitter, was nothing short of remarkable.

To me, the nagging question was not just why so many people and organizations were willing to override fundamental democratic principles in order to show that they were on the "right side" of an issue. It was why the threat of danger on campus remained so compelling. Why were so many people so invested in the idea that women on college campuses or anywhere else are subject to male predatory behavior at practically every turn? If George Will was wholly and despicably wrongheaded to suggest that victimhood might on some level have a few perks, why do so many young women seem so willing to recast unpleasant or regrettable sex into violative sex? What are they getting out of it? Is there something more intrinsically satisfying about seeing yourself as a victim/survivor rather than a normal human capable of making mistakes that might result in unpleasant situations that leave you feeling icky for a while?

"If the alcohol is out and you're in a room with a bunch of progressive social justice warriors who are women, someone's going to start talking about sexual assault. My theory is that other people are kind of encouraged to share their own stories of being assaulted, whether or not these stories may be true."

This is Toni Airaksinen, who graduated from Barnard College in 2018 and with whom I had a series of conversations while writing this book. At the time of our first conversation, she was twenty years old and wrapping up her sophomore year. I discovered Toni through her articles for the Columbia University student newspaper, which showed a good-natured, fair-minded resistance to the left-leaning party line. She wrote about speech codes (she was against them) and men's studies classes (she was for them). It was never inflammatory, just conspicuously against the grain.

"I believe that our collective concern over microaggressions is infantilizing and detrimental and that we should definitely not have a microaggression reporting system," she wrote in the *Columbia Daily Spectator* in the fall of 2016.

When I contacted Toni in the early stages of working on this book (after having read her *Spectator* pieces), I assumed she was a member of the College Libertarians or at least some kind of flinty Alex P. Keaton type, rebelling from a crunchy bourgeois upbringing by pushing back against political correctness and liberal sanctimony. But what I found was the complete opposite, which in retrospect makes perfect sense.

She grew up in inner city Cleveland in a poor family that received food stamps. Neither of her parents graduated from high school, and her mother, as Toni describes her, was "a very violent person," from whom Toni and her younger sister are now legally independent. Toni managed to get herself into a public high school that had a dual-enrollment program with Cleveland State University, and she took buses and subways two hours in each direction every day to attend this school. She knew she was "bad in math and science, the things that make money," and as a result wasn't hung up on taking STEM classes the way a lot of kids trying to climb out of poverty might be. Instead her classes at Cleveland State included several women's studies courses, and here she "drank the feminist Kool-Aid," she says.

While commuting to school, she says, she probably got catcalled and harassed on the street at least a dozen times a day. She grew up in neighborhoods where this was a constant, so she never gave it much thought. At least not until she took women's studies class.

"Someone saying 'Hey, beautiful' to you as you walk by them on the street, the chances that they're going to lunge at you and attack you with a knife is almost zero percent," Toni told me. "So you just kind of shrug your shoulders or smile or say things back to them or whatever. I never felt like it was a problem until I got to Cleveland State and they were teaching us that the patriarchy is everywhere. They taught us that street harassment is a sign of male oppression trying to keep women afraid. They taught us that Subway advertisements were sexist because they used the phallic image of the sub sandwich to sell their sandwiches."

Toni told me she was on board for these lessons. She became active in social justice causes around LGBT issues, having identified as a lesbian since early adolescence. She began dating men in college and suspects her previous gay identification was due at least partly to the Tumblr sites she followed in high school, which made being gay seem like the cool and social justice–minded thing to be. She applied to more than a dozen out-of-state colleges and chose Columbia University's Barnard College because it offered enough scholarships and financial aid so she could attend debt free. Once she got there she became involved in a student organization that lobbied for resources for first-generation college students. It was 2014, the year a senior named Emma Sulkowicz was lugging her mattress everywhere she went in protest of the university's decision not to expel a fellow student who Sulkowicz said had raped her. Classmates routinely showed their support by helping carry the mattress as they crossed paths with Sulkowicz, and Toni pitched in a few times. For her sophomore year, she applied for residency in Social Justice House, a dormitory for like-minded student activists.

"I thought it would be great to go, and so I went," she said. "And then I got cannibalized alive."

The incidents, as described, pile up so fast and from so many directions that Toni sometimes seemed to be skidding across them rather than recounting them. Though she claims she was active in urban relief and anti-poverty work and, as such, was the only one among her four suite mates who was doing "legitimate activism" rather than "armchair social justice," she soon became targeted as problematic. For starters, there were the articles she was now writing for the *Spectator*, opinion pieces that, despite her self-professed commitment to liberal ideals, had headlines like "Rape Culture and the Problem with the 1 in 5 Sexual Assault Statistic" and "Lift the Ban on Student-Professor Relationships." Then there was the stuff she posted on Facebook: for instance, an article by conservative *New York Post* columnist Naomi Schaefer Riley suggesting that campuses didn't have a rape problem as much as a drinking problem. She was also sharing articles by libertarian writers like Cathy Young and Robby Soave, who were considered personae non gratae by many of her classmates.

Later there was the suite mate who didn't get out of bed for several days and, according to Toni, took Toni's offer to get her orange juice or cough drops as a racist microaggression.

"Maybe a few weeks later, she came back to me and said that because I had commented on the fact that she was in bed all day I was reinforcing the stereotype of people of color as lazy," Toni told me. "She literally used the word 'microaggressing.' And by then there was this idea that people did not feel safe with me living in the suite because of the articles I wrote and the things I posted on social media. They were saying things to each other on Facebook like 'I have an air mattress in case anyone needs to not sleep in the same room as Toni because Toni supports rape culture.'"

Toni said she managed to keep her cool enough to not respond to the Facebook messages, but that occasionally students would approach her in person when she was working at her job at the front desk of the student center. She said she generally tried to avoid confrontation by saying things like "Sorry, I can't talk now" or "Just shoot me a message on Facebook if you want to peacefully chat." (She thinks maybe one person took her up on it.) At one point, she said, enough students had complained that her writing amounted to violations of the group rules of Social Justice House that she had to meet with a Residence Life officer.

"I was fearful during that time," she recalled. "Mostly of just completely losing my housing."

It's worth noting that, during this period, the tone of the rape-culture conversation at Columbia had been set by Sulkowicz, whose mattress project was by then an international symbol of campus anti-rape activism. In 2013, Sulkowicz had filed a complaint against Paul Nungesser, a former friend with whom she periodically had sex, accusing him of forcibly sod-omizing her and trying to choke her eight months earlier (the encounter had begun consensually but turned violent, she said). Columbia adjudicated the case and eventually cleared Nungesser of all charges. Sulkowicz subsequently filed a po-lice report against Nungesser, but the district attorney found "lack of reasonable suspicion" and the case was not pursued.

Unsatisfied with this verdict, Sulkowicz announced that she would carry her fifty-pound mattress on her back—from classroom to dining hall to dormitory—until Nungesser was expelled. An art major, she arranged to turn the endeavor into her thesis project, a piece of performance art called *Carry That Weight*. Over the year she carried the mattress, classmates routinely pitched in and helped her. Meanwhile, she appeared on the cover of *New York* magazine, the storied performance artist Marina Abramovic praised her, and art critic Jerry Saltz named the project one of the best art shows of the year, say-ing it "may make universities think twice before looking past the plight of women." Soon the mattress moved beyond the realm of art and became the symbol of a movement, as women at colleges all over the country took to carrying their pillows in a show of solidarity.

The idea that one in five women will be sexually assaulted during her time in college is by now an article of faith. It comes up routinely in the media, in activist communities, and, of course, on campuses themselves. President Obama and Vice President Biden cited the statistic repeatedly as they launched the "It's On Us" public awareness campaign around campus sexual violence in 2014. As Biden memorably and dramatically put it, "We know the numbers: one in five of every one of those young women who is dropped off for that first day of school, before they finish school, will be assaulted, will be assaulted in her college years."

I like Joe Biden well enough (not necessarily enough to be the next president), but this is misleading at best and propagandistic at worst. Presumably he did not know—or chose to overlook for the purposes of narrative—the fact that the statistic is based on surveys taken in 2006 for a National Institute of Justice study called *The Campus Sexual Assault Study*. Respondents came from just two universities, and the questions were worded in such a way that "assault" could mean anything from forcible penetration to "unwanted sexual touching," which could include something like getting groped at a crowded fraternity party (a punishable offense, but hardly the kind of assault that should be counted with rape).

But just as there will probably never be a consensus as to the origin of the phrase "lies, damn lies, and statistics" (even though Mark Twain popularized it in his line about "three kinds of lies," it's been attributed to everyone from British statesmen to various newspaper journalists), it's unlikely there will ever be a set of agreed-upon figures about campus rape. In 2015, an Association of American Universities survey narrowed the Justice Department's one-in-five statistic to an even more alarming one in four. To confuse matters even further, a 2014 report from the Justice Department, this one focusing on violent crime, showed that between 1995 and 2013 the rate of rape or sexual assault among female college students was around closer to one in forty-one. That report, incidentally, showed that violent crime was on the decline across the board and also that females who were not enrolled in college were statistically at greater risk than those who were.

The numbers can be parsed and massaged and spun for ideological purposes all day. This is especially the case because, again, many of the surveys, especially those with ratios like one in four and one in five, define assault as anything from forcible rape to an unwanted kiss to sexual activity when one or both parties are technically too drunk to consent. That last concept is, in and of itself, so subjective and abstract that it would seem like the opposite of anything that could be "defined." While everyone would agree that people who are intoxicated to the point of obvious physical or mental impairment are no more able to consent to sex than they are able to safely operate a motor vehicle, what about people who are mildly intoxicated?

What about those one or two or sometimes three drinks that a lot of perfectly well-functioning, cognitively mature grown-ups require (or at least wouldn't turn down) before venturing into a sexual encounter with someone new? What about the significant portion of college students who have blackouts while drinking? They can behave normally and appear to be in control of their faculties and yet wake up the next morning with no memory of what happened (a Duke University study estimated that 51 percent of students who drink alcohol have experienced this at least once). Are would-be bedfellows supposed to pull out ophthalmoscopes to examine one another's pupils in order to gauge the legitimacy of apparent sexual willingness? (And would that even work?) Are drunk men any more able to give consent than drunk women and, if not, why do most campus adjudication processes hold the male more responsible for his actions than the female for hers, even if he may have been the more intoxicated party?

Back at the University of Iowa, Joseph got lucky in the end, at least relatively speaking. Though he was initially barred from entering any classroom that his accuser was in—and this kept him from attending several lectures and taking several exams—he was eventually placed on non-academic probation for an entire calendar year. He was never told exactly what he was accused of and never faced his accuser in any formal hearing. He did, however, receive a forty-page report from the assistant dean of students. In an e-mail to me, Joseph described this report as a statement of "all the evidence from all angles of my case, which to my surprise contained some evidence that consisted of research he even did on his own."

Joseph wasn't able to share that report or tell me much of the details, but in his e-mail he told me how hard it was to be barred from extracurricular activities, because "my status really held me back from securing roles on campus that I was offered." All in all, though, he was doing great. He loved studying engineering and was involved in engineering clubs and conservative political organizations. Best of all, he said,

"I have a wonderful girlfriend (together for 6 months today!) who knows me, my story, and what I stand for and treats me better than I could ever be asked to be treated."

I wish I could have interviewed the woman who had this experience with Joseph. I understand why he can't give me her name or put me in contact with her, even for an anonymous chat. Even if he weren't under strict administrative orders not to share any information about her, it would make sense that he'd want to protect her privacy, if only not to stir up any more trouble. But I hate that I can't get her side of the story. I don't like that I've had to refer to her as Joseph's "accuser" while re-laying what he told me. That word feels impersonal and judg-mental, as if the accuser is actually the accused.

But when details are withheld, even for good reason, vo-cabulary can be found wanting. I wish there was a way I could more emphatically convey just how much empathy I have for this woman who, for whatever reason, left that dorm that night apparently feeling much different than she had when she entered. Knowing Joseph personally may allow me to give him some benefit of the doubt, but I'm almost certain that if it had been the woman I'd met first, her story would have equal or possibly greater resonance. As it is, even though I've only met one of them, I essentially believe both of them. I believe the woman had the experience of things going terribly wrong and I believe Joseph had the experience of things just being a little awkward. I could be mistaken either way. But if there's anything to be learned here, it's that mistakes aren't often quantifiable.

In lieu of interviewing Joseph's accuser, I could have interviewed dozens if not hundreds of women who've had similar experiences. They're not hard to find. Whatever statistic you favor about the rate of sexual assault on campus, one in five or one in forty-one, that's still an enormous number of women. But I didn't feel it was the place or purview of this book to include survivors' stories just for the sake of including them. Their stories are everywhere. They are in news reports, in online spaces, in Take Back the Night rallies, at your kitchen table when you're sitting across from a female friend or family member (if you bother to ask her). Some are harrowing accounts involving fraternity rituals that aim to get women inebriated (or in some cases drugged without their knowledge) to the point of incapacitation so that they can be taken advantage of. In spring 2019, it was reported that Swarthmore College in Pennsylvania, a school typically regarded as a bastion of bookish eggheads, was home to a so-called "rape attic" in a fraternity house. This is to say nothing of the countless fraternity-related sexual assaults reported every year at large state universities, where student athletes sometimes get a free pass and a celebrated culture of hard partying masks a more insidious culture of objectifying and violating women.

I could go on. And on. But that would only serve to repeat what we already know—that the social and sexual lives of college students can be profoundly vulnerable and any response to trouble therein is bound to be imperfect—sometimes in ways that only compound the harm already done. Parents themselves make tons of errors in judgment, and so do college administrations acting in loco parentis. What I will say about Joseph is that I'm inclined to think not that he did anything technically wrong—at least if his story is true—as much as he just didn't do things quite right. Regardless of a guy's virginity status or facility with a condom, ejaculating inside a woman (either by accident or out of indifference) who hasn't given you explicit permission to do so is bad news. Any woman who's had this happen to her (and my estimate would put that at roughly in the range of "many to most") knows that it's sub-optimal at best and a catastrophe at worst. But it's not assault, at least not in my mind.

For some reason, the detail that stays with me most about Joseph's story is the image of the young woman repeatedly craning her neck around and looking at him expectantly while they're watching the movie. It stays with me because I've pulled that move, as no doubt many women have. It's not one that belongs in the dignity column, but when you find yourself eager for physical intimacy from a guy who seems disinclined to make the first move, looking at him expectantly is prac-tically an automatic reflex. The snapping shut of the laptop and subsequent nuclear option of saying "You don't get it, do you?" would never have been in my arsenal, but I can imagine *imagining* that it was.

I can imagine wondering what it would be like to be the kind of woman who can finesse such a move. I can imagine running through all the possible outcomes to such a move: he could recoil, he could get immediately turned on, he could fall in love with me by night's end, he could dredge this story up while giving a drunken toast at our wedding while I feign mortification and also secretly congratulate myself on the badass move that started it all. I can imagine none of those outcomes coming to fruition but instead going home that night feeling awkward and embarrassed and suddenly worried about being pregnant. I can imagine feeling angry about this new worry, so angry in fact that I feel justified in asking the guy to pay for emergency contraception. What I cannot imagine is reporting him to the university administration for sexual misconduct.

In parsing why that is, I realized that perhaps the starkest difference between Generation X and the generations that are now or were recently in college lies in the soul of our self-definition. We were obsessed with being tough. They are obsessed with being fair. Just as "life in the big city" loomed large in our imaginations, life in a better world looms in theirs. Which of these outlooks is more likely to end in disappointment I could not presume to say. If anything, they may be different paths to the same destination: regular old, complicated adulthood. We all get there one way or another.

CHAPTER 6

On the Right Side of Things
(Until I Wasn't)

My first taste of the sweet rewards of what would come to be known as virtue signaling came in 1994, when I wrote an essay about Take Our Daughters to Work Day. The essay emerged out of a workshop in my graduate-school writing program and was notable less for its subject matter than for its style, which was very much in the Joan Didion knockoff vein. In addition to having a lot of adverbs and run-on sentences, it was a little bit sanctimonious and a lot snarky—even though "snarky" wasn't a word anyone used back then. It was the essay that made me realize I was an essayist (up until then I'd been a writer of unmemorable short stories in the Lorrie Moore knockoff vein). Even as I was writing the first draft, I knew it was a departure; I remember literally tingling as I sat at my Mac Quadra computer, the screen saver occasionally flipping on and displaying a galaxy of animated flying toasters.

The essay wasn't entirely coherent from a logic stand-point, but it had enough zing that it became my signature work for the better part of a year. I used it to enter contests and apply for various conferences, including a particularly prestigious one in Vermont that granted me a full scholarship. The conference included a daily workshop. Ideally I would have submitted new work for critique, but I recycled my same pages yet again.

The opening scene of the essay was the first ever Take Our Daughters to Work Day, on April 22, 1993. Established by the Ms. Foundation for Women and changed in 2003 to Take Our Daughters and Sons to Work Day, this initiative was all about making girls aware of the myriad professional oppor-tunities available to them. It was about reminding them that they were more valuable than their looks and their homemak-ing skills. To that end, girls were taken on field trips to par-ticipating workplaces across the country (read: white-collar offices staffed by parents, relatives, and friends thereof) and shown what futures lay in store for them if only they did well in school and eschewed early marriage and motherhood for Anne Klein power suits and commuter Nikes.

I was working at the beauty magazine at the time, where makeup samples choked the cubicles the way legal briefs pile up at law firms. When, around midmorning on April 22, a group of girls showed up in our midst (I had no idea who they belonged to, since practically no one on staff had children), they were not given a tour of the art department or explained the magic of the fax machine but instead shepherded directly into the conference room. There, piles of lip-gloss tubes and foundation compacts lay in wait along with a handful of low-level assistants who'd been tasked with "making over" the young guests. It seemed that any time spent observing their fellow females hard at work in wage-earning, high-skilled jobs (which in my case required calling the Frédéric Fekkai hair salon multiple times a day to reschedule my boss's appointments) would be literally overshadowed by MAC glitter shadow.

My essay, which I'd entitled, in a nod to Henny Youngman, "Take Our Daughters," explored the *irony* of all of this. It talked about the interworkings of the magazine and its place within a large and powerful family of other glossy magazines, most aimed at women. It talked about what it was like to work in the female-dominated environment of this big company. It talked about the Seven Sisters college from which I had graduated just weeks before starting my job and (this is where the logic began to founder) the ways the Seven Sisters and this magazine company shared a contrasting but also oddly similar feminist legacy. I think I tried to say something about how "female empowerment" (thanks to my Didion thievery, I put a lot of things in quotes) had been turned into a brand. I talked about the hypocrisy of a women's movement that was willing to perpetuate oppressive beauty rituals as long as those rituals were being presented under the mantle of "feminism," i.e., girls getting makeovers on Take Our Daughters to Work Day. I wrote "i.e." a lot.

The prestigious writers conference to which this essay had

gained me entry included the chance to give a reading before all the attendees. Up until the time of this reading, I had been known to most of the attendees as nothing more than one of the ten scholarship holders whose duty it was to wait tables in exchange for room and board. But when I joined my fellow waiters in a presentation of our work and read a five-minute excerpt from "Take Our Daughters," my profile soared in the space of those five minutes.

In its simplified and shortened form, the essay sounded like an easily digestible, automatically respectable feminist tract: *Beauty magazines, bad! Girl power, good!* With shaky hands but a strong voice, I stood at a podium in a converted barn and delivered my righteous prose. That is to say, I read seven hundred or so words that, thanks to the abbreviated context, sounded a lot more righteous than they really were. In spite of the choking heat inside the rustic performance space, the audience applauded vigorously. The next day, as I waited my tables, I for once was met not with complaints about the undercooked vegetables but with praise for my politics.

"You're really on the right side of things," a man with floppy, silver-flecked hair said to me. "Important stuff you're doing."

"Amazing work," said a woman wearing jangly silver bracelets. "So essential. So brave."

An agent gave me his card. A book editor said to call her if I ever had any book ideas. Someone told me I sounded like Joan Didion.

I lapped up the compliments. I also knew deep down that they were rote responses to what, in the five minutes' worth of material I'd presented, amounted to extremely obvious ideas. I'd spooned up a serving of highly legible liberalism and been rewarded accordingly. It was the intellectual version of a cheap high.

Almost twenty years later, Twitter would make this sort of conditioned response transaction available on a moment-to-moment basis. But back then, it felt like a special occasion, albeit one I knew not to trust, like being invited to the birthday party of someone you know doesn't like you all that much. Sometimes I wonder if my resistance was to my detriment. I probably could have written an entire book saying *Beauty magazines, bad! Girl power, good!* and made a more lucrative career for myself than the one I ended up making. But doing so would have felt as counterfeit as that five-minute reading at the conference, the journalistic version of never coming out of the closet.

For what it's worth, Didion herself had no truck with ideologies that were fashionable for fashion's sake. Few seem to remember it now, but back in 1972 Didion pretty much declared herself a conscientious objector in the feminist wars. "To make an omelet, you need not only those broken eggs but somebody 'oppressed' to break them," she wrote in the *New York Times Book Review*. The essay, called, simply, "The Women's Movement" (and which was later included in her collection *The White Album*), drew from some fifteen books dealing with the fraught sexual politics of the era; authors ranged from Simone de Beauvoir to Shulamith Firestone to Germaine Greer to Norman Mailer. Didion resisted "the invention of women as a class" and, moreover, chafed at the way "this ubiquitous construct" had been assigned a narrative rooted chiefly in victimology.

> She was persecuted even by her gynecologist, who made her beg in vain for contraceptives. She particularly needed contraceptives because she was raped on every date, raped by her husband, and raped, finally, on the abortionist's table. During the fashion for shoes with pointed toes she, like "many women," had her toes amputated . . .
>
> The half-truths, repeated, authenticated themselves. The bitter fancies assumed their own logic. To ask the obvious—why she did not get herself another gynecologist, another job, why she did not get out of bed and turn off the television set, or why, the most eccentric detail, she stayed in hotels where only doughnuts could be obtained from room service—was to join this argument at its own spooky level, a level which had only the most tenuous and unfortunate relationship to the actual condition of being a woman.

Whoa there, Saint Joan! Can you even begin to imagine what would happen if such words were published today? Can you imagine the outrage that would ensue if some vigilante tweeter dug up the *Times* archive of this article and posted a link to it along with an incredulous "WTF" or "I Can't Even"— or, better yet, some GIF of Betty White looking perplexed? (The term for this practice is now "outrage archaeology.") *Get another gynecologist? Get another job? What kind of bullshit inter-*

nalized misogyny is this? What kind of problematic privileged white critique of problematic privileged white feminism are you peddling here? Amiright?

Back in the day, the usual suspects got their noses out of joint. *Ms.* magazine, which at the time single-handedly did the job that Jezebel, Dame, Bustle, *Teen Vogue*, Everyday Feminism, and a thousand Tumblr accounts do today, rushed in with a critique as readily as firefighters holding a life net outside the window of a burning building. Didion's "attitudes pose a problem to all of us," wrote the feminist scholar Catharine Stimpson in a *Ms.* article titled "The Case of Miss Joan Didion" (note the cheeky honorific). Stimpson attacked the premise that feminism, at least in its current iteration, was a fundamentally adolescent expression, "a familiar anti-feminist strategy." This premise, Stimpson wrote, was "too inaccurate, too obvious when it was accurate, and too smug to be taken seriously."

Nearly half a century later, Didion is a goddess among not just second-wave but also third- and fourth-wave feminists. Her name appears reliably on lists like "Badass Women of History" and "11 Times Joan Didion Was the Coolest Writer of All Time." In 2015, just months after two pairs of sunglasses Didion had owned were offered up for $2,500 each as part of a Kickstarter campaign to fund a documentary about her life, Didion appeared in an ad for the fashion company Celine's spring collection.

But young people who first encountered Didion as a stunned and grieving widow in *The Year of Magical Thinking*, and, digging a little deeper, discovered crowd-pleasers like her signature essay "Goodbye to All That," might be surprised to know that in 1962 a twenty-eight-year-old Didion said that California gubernatorial candidate Richard Nixon was "too liberal" for her taste. She was an enthusiastic supporter of Barry Goldwater when he was the Republican nominee for president in 1964 and she wrote for the *National Review* throughout much of that decade. Though Didion became more liberal as time went on, her feminism was more implicit than it was overt; it was certainly never performative. She dismissed political activism among Hollywood liberals as a "kind of dictatorship of good intentions" characterized by a "vacant fervor." She called out virtue signaling before there was a name for it.

For the last few years, I don't think a single day has passed when I haven't wondered what Joan Didion at the height of her powers would have to say about the political and intellectual state of America today. What could she do with twelve thousand words in the *New York Review of Books* on white privilege, on rape culture, on campus speech issues, on #MeToo? What would she make of the ways in which the vacant fervor of glamorous activism has only grown more vacant and fervent over the decades? What would she say about Robert De Niro shouting "Fuck Trump" at the Tony Awards ceremony in 2018? Of the #OscarsSoWhite movement in 2016? Of Patricia Arquette, in 2015, accepting the Oscar for best supporting actress and making some platitudinous remarks about wage equality that had Meryl Streep (a Vassar grad and one of my personal heroes) practically leaping from her seat as she pointed to Arquette in "you go, girl" approval? (This image has become a hugely popular GIF, frequently deployed as a signal of approval among badass feminists on social media.)

What would Didion have thought when, two years after Arquette's battle cry on the Oscars stage, the actress was part of a chorus of social media outrage over what came to be known as "leggingsgate"?

In case you've forgotten—or missed it the first time—#leggingsgate refers to a minor atrocity committed by a United Airlines gate agent who refused to let a pair of teenage girls board a flight in Denver because they were wearing leggings in lieu of pants. The reason was that the girls were traveling with their parents on employee buddy passes. Employee buddy passes allow passengers who have friends or family who work for the airline to fly for free or at a deep discount. In exchange, these passengers are asked to adhere to a dress code. (There was a time when that meant coat and tie for men.) United's dress code for buddy passes prohibited a range of commonly worn street clothes, including "form-fitting lycra/spandex tops, pants, and dresses."

According to reports (by which I mean official news reports as well as the random tweets of random people), a gate agent in Denver informed the family of the buddy-pass dress policy. By all appearances, the family was cooperative and attempted some sort of improvisatory wardrobe change (a younger girl, also in leggings, was allowed to wear them if she put a dress on over them). But a woman named Shannon Watts happened to be standing nearby and watching it all go down, at least as far as she could see from her place in line for another flight.

Apparently unaware of the full details of the situation, Watts took the liberty of firing off a string of tweets offering her interpretation as she saw it from some distance away. Her interpretation was that the airline was "policing the clothing of women and girls." United's public relations department responded with some tweets about proper attire, not making it sufficiently clear they were talking about the very specific dress code associated with a little-known travel perk. This—and the fact that Watts happened to be a prominent anti-gun activist with a fairly large Twitter following—stirred up enough foment that a number of celebrities entered the fray, among them Arquette.

"The highest standard of any culture corporate or not is to allow children to be children and dress in accordance," Arquette tweeted.

A short time later, Arquette added, "Leggings are business attire for 10 year olds. Their business is being children."

The model Chrissy Teigen soon joined in. "I have flown united before with literally no pants on. Just a top as a dress. Next time I will only wear jeans and a scarf."

William Shatner tweeted a shot of himself, from a *Star Trek* episode, shirtless and wearing leggings emblazoned with the Starfleet arrow symbol. The comedian Billy Eichner joked about how he'd flown with his penis exposed and had no problems, adding the hashtag #Misogyny for good measure. Even when the whole concept behind buddy passes and dress codes finally began to seep in, the Twittersphere would not part with its outrage. Comedian Sarah Silverman went through the motions of trying to reason with the company in text speak—"I understand. I suggest u consider updating ur rules 4 friends & fam as they seem to apply mostly 2 females & are outdated"—and actor Seth Rogen took the opportunity to just flat-out virtue signal: "We here @united are just trying to police the attire of the daughters of our employees! That's all! Cool, right?"

The tweets became their own news stories, with outlets from *People* magazine to the *Washington Post* whipping up half-baked yet hyperventilating posts about United's misogyny. Watts herself managed to post an opinion article on Time.com the very next day, entitled "I'm the Woman Who Called Out United and I'm Sick of Sexism."

> Women are tired of being policed for our clothing. Dress codes are laced with words and phrases that easily conform to—and are manipulated by—a misogynist society. United's pass rider dress policy, whether intentional or not, is sexist, and it sexualizes young girls by calling their leggings inappropriate.
>
> As a woman and a mom of five kids, I was uncomfortable and angered by what unfolded at the Denver airport.

#Leggingsgate was hardly the signature internet scolding event of the season. It probably wasn't even the biggest one of the week. (Nearly two years later, the fundamental mechanics of the whole donnybrook would play themselves out on a much bigger and more serious scale in the form of a viral video that led to the hounding of MAGA hat–wearing high school students who had been deemed racists for no rational or coherent reason.) But for some reason, the story obsessed me. It wasn't just that I've always been peevish about overly casual dress on airplanes and generally think airline personnel are among the most unfairly maligned workers in the labor force. It wasn't just that I wished United's buddy-pass dress code, which also prohibited "attire that reveals any type of undergarments" and "attire that is designated as sleepwear, underwear or swim attire," applied to all commercial passengers on all airlines at all times. (I've long been convinced that approximately a third of all passengers flying in and out of LAX are wearing sweatpants with the word "Juicy" written across the butt.) It was that the sanctimony sickened me. The chorus of scolding had built to such a crescendo that pretty soon it wasn't even a chorus anymore—just part of the white noise of online life itself. Pretty soon, I felt there wouldn't be any point in saying anything. Pretty soon, I felt, there would be just two lanes on the conversation highway: the one in which everyone agreed to agree, no matter the truth, and the one in which you're inaudible.

Half-truths, repeated, authenticate themselves. After twenty-five years as a working writer, I can't believe what's happened to words themselves. It's as if they've been starved of oxygen.

It's as if they've been denied one another's company, forced into a solitary confinement in which their value is based solely on their most basic definitions. Robbed of context, flattened into blunt objects, they thrash about, unmoored, in the seas of stupidity, only to crash so hard on the rocks that they break apart into further meaninglessness.

Sexism. Misogyny. White supremacy. What do these words even mean now? What is justice? What is rage? What is privilege? Why have we decided that prejudice against some groups is phobic—transphobia, homophobia, Islamophobia, xenophobia—and prejudice against other groups is just prejudice? What is "My feminism will be intersectional or it will be bullshit" even supposed to mean? It originated as the title of a 2011 manifesto-like essay by feminist writer Flavia Dzodan, but even Dzodan has bucked at its watering down. In 2016 she wrote a Medium essay entitled "My feminism will be capitalist, appropriative, bullshit merchandise." She may be onto something.

The theory of intersectionality was coined and first discussed in 1989 by law professor Kimberlé Crenshaw, who was then at UCLA and has been at Columbia University Law School since 1995. Originally used in the context of a 1976 anti-discrimination case involving black female workers suing General Motors, it refers to a framework for looking at how privilege and oppression play out in cultural cross sections. On its face, intersectionality always seemed to me an entirely reasonable and useful schema for thinking about the world. It's important to understand that, for instance, a white woman can

experience sexist discrimination because she's a woman and, all the while, a black woman can be discriminated against on sexist *and* racist fronts. Similarly, even though men may, generally speaking, be considered the privileged sex, black men have a double disadvantage because in some situations their blackness may compound stereotypes related to their masculinity (in that sense, black women may in some situations have an advantage over black men). Intersectional analysis also takes into account factors like disability, sexual orientation, gender identity, and various other forms of social stratification.

In theory (and intersectionality is just that, a theory) this all sounds great. The problem is that intersectionality has been subject to gross misapplication. From there, it's been oversimplified and sensationalized. In the worst cases, it's used as an excuse for the kind of circular firing squad you see when one sort of marginalized person tries to pull rank against another. No longer just a framework, it's now a doctrine in which group identities are assigned value based on the amount of discrimination its members are likely to experience. This interpretation has given way to what the anti-PC crowd likes to call the Oppression Olympics; the more disadvantaged you are because of prejudices aimed at your particular group, the more deserving you are of reparations. In that sense (and in ways that range from the patently obvious to the largely incomprehensible), intersectionality gets tangled up in things like Marxism and postmodernism.

Intersectionality has been all the rage on college campuses for the last decade at least. But sometime around the midway

point of Barack Obama's second term, maybe late 2014, I noticed it was beginning to wander off the campus and into the mainstream media sphere. Here, the framework for actual thinking mutated into a framework for the shorthand thinking of virtue signaling. The seductions of this shorthand were obvious; there was no need to sort out facts or wrestle with contradictions when just using certain buzzwords— patriarchy, white supremacy, gaslighting—would grant automatic entry into a group of ostensibly like-minded peers. Inside this group, the narrative was already established and solidarity was assumed: *Ironic feminist memes, good; mansplaining, bad! Black Lives Matter, good; unchecked white privilege, bad!* And since this group contained an enormous generational demographic, the millennials, the trend spotters in the media smartly figured out that the way to reach them was by speaking their language, the language of virtue signaling. The way to reach them was to take intersectionality, which had already been turned into a trend, and make it into the ultimate brand.

From there, the brand could be wielded as a weapon against ideological opponents. If, for instance, you suggested that (or even wondered aloud if) the gender wage gap might not be entirely due to systemic sexism but also to women's interests, choices, and the inconvenient but unavoidable realities of pregnancy and rearing young children, you were likely to be labeled an internalized misogynist. This same dynamic played out in other spheres of public debate, too: gun control, immigration, due process in campus sexual assault cases. If you more or less toed the requisite liberal line but thought there were some gray areas that warranted consideration, you were on the wrong side of history. If you called for nuance, you were part of the problem.

This dynamic started feeling really acute around 2015, maybe even a little bit before. And it wasn't just in the media sphere. I also began to sense some fraying around the edges of my social circles. Both online and in real life, people who'd once shared a common set of assumptions about the realities of the world and the nature of human behavior now seemed divided. Questions that had once been treated as complicated inquiries were increasingly being reduced to moral absolutes, at least as far as liberal types were concerned.

By the summer of 2018, amid that roiling debate between what you might call the civility camp versus the outrage camp of the Trump resistance, "nuance" had become a kind of fighting word. For civility types, who feared that displays of indiscriminate and unfettered rage against the Trump regime were as strategically misguided as they were viscerally satisfying, nuance was what was sorely lacking. In the outrage camp, the call for nuance was sometimes seen as a form of tone policing, a dog whistle for centrist and right-leaning scolds whose privilege blinded them to the severity of the crisis before them. Both sides had a point (naturally).

As the summer sputtered along, I was struck by how much this state of cultural cognitive dissonance resembled the developing situation inside my brain over the last few years: a situation best described as a maddening toggle between what I felt versus what I thought I was supposed to feel.

What I thought I was supposed to feel probably has its roots in one of my earliest political memories: seeing the devastation on my parents' faces as Walter Cronkite showed an electoral map blotted with Ronald Reagan's landslide win in the 1980 presidential election. My parents, pro-union liberals who'd been raised in coal country and later shaped by the values and sensibilities of academia, weren't especially political. My mother might have sat on the Capitol steps rallying for the ERA, but she wasn't out canvassing or glued to the news. Nonetheless, my parents had instilled in me the standard set of middle-class Democratic Party values: public safety nets were a force for good, corporate greed was a real threat, civil and reproductive rights were paramount. I carried these values with me to college, where they blended right in with just about everyone else's. When George H. W. Bush was elected president in 1988, students wrote "moving to Canada" in thick Magic Marker on their bedsheets and hung the sheets from dorm windows.

I've never voted for a Republican in my life. The decade-plus I spent as a newspaper opinion columnist tapped into my penchant for devil's advocacy (*Hey, why* shouldn't *Sarah Palin call herself a feminist?*) and I enjoyed getting angry letters from liberals almost as much as I enjoyed getting them from conservatives. But for the most part, I spent the bulk of my adulthood essentially aligned with the kinds of people I'd gone to college with. That we were all on the same team was simply a given. We all read the *New York Times*, listened to NPR, and voted for Democrats. We would all go to the mat for women's rights, gay rights, or pretty much any rights other than gun rights. We lived, for the most part, in big cities in blue states. When Barack Obama appeared on the scene, we loved him with the delirium of crushed-out teenagers, perhaps less for his policies than for being the kind of person who also listens to NPR. We loved Hillary Clinton with the fraught resignation of daughters' love for their mothers. We loved her even if we didn't like her. We were liberals after all. We were family.

Maybe it was the impending loss of Obama that caused us to begin this unconscious process of detachment—from one another as well as from him. Maybe we knew we'd never be in love like this again, so bit by bit, we started looking for problems, picking fights, finding the dissatisfaction that had apparently been hiding deep inside our contentment. It wasn't hard, since injustices large and small were in the foreground of our daily lives like never before. Cell phone cameras, now ubiquitous, left no public altercation undocumented. Screen shots left no ill-advised text or tweet permanently unarchived. "Social justice warriors" emerged on the scene with a self-proclaimed utopian vision that sometimes sounded a lot like authoritarianism. Social media, the narcotic we were already all addicted to, now did double duty as an outrage amplifier and disseminator of half-truths spoken by well-meaning but unreliable narrators.

Some of my best friends were such narrators. On Facebook and Twitter, their posts rang out with equal measure of passion and paranoia. For all their sophistication and critical thinking skills—these were people with advanced degrees and *New Yorker* subscriptions—more than a few of them were coming across as surprisingly closed-minded. A link to an inflammatory article about college sexual assault would set off a cascade of Facebook comments about being afraid to send daughters to leafy liberal arts colleges that were surely teeming with violent predators. A comment expressing even mild sympathy for the obvious psychological troubles of someone like Rachel Dolezal, the white woman who was publicly shamed for pretending to be black, would be smacked down as an example of unchecked white privilege or even unabashed white supremacy. And these weren't just meme-crazed youngsters flouting their newly minted knowledge of intersectional theory. Many were in their forties and fifties, posting photos from their kids' middle school graduations along with rage-filled jeremiads about toxic masculinity. And here they were, adopting the vocabulary of Tumblr, typing things like *I. Just. Cant. With. This*. One afternoon, following a perfectly pleasant lunch near the beach in Los Angeles, I practically got into a shouting match with a close friend about whether, as she put it, "the world sucked for women." Her conviction was that it obviously did. My feeling was that she and I must at some point have stopped living in the same world. In the ensuing months I had different versions of this same conversation with several other friends. I began to feel very lonely.

Herein is where, slowly and strangely, I started to make some new friends. Though they often weren't discernibly on one particular side or another, I reliably felt that they were on my side. I began to find them in early 2015 on YouTube.

This was before Trump even entered the political picture. I found the first ones specifically through Bloggingheads.tv, a low-tech video blogging site where scholars and journalists of all ideological stripes carried on webcam conversations about the issues of the day. I was a particular fan of the monthly dialogue between the economist and professor Glenn Loury and the linguist and literature professor John McWhorter. Calling themselves "the black guys on Bloggingheads.tv," they talked about racial politics with more candor and (ahem) *nuance* than I'd probably ever heard in my life. They even dared to do what few in the left-leaning chatterati were willing to do: hold the writer Ta-Nehisi Coates up to scrutiny. Often it wasn't so much the author himself that they griped about but the rote, self-congratulatory reverence displayed by Coates's white fans. This reverence was itself racist, McWhorter pointed out. "The elevation of that kind of dorm-lounge performance art as serious thought is a kind of soft bigotry which is as nauseating as it is unintended," he said.

This delighted me. For months I'd been trying, much less eloquently, to make this same point to anyone who'd listen, which was nobody. I had read Coates and learned a lot from him. But with this reading often came the nagging sense that I wasn't supposed to engage with the ideas as much as absorb them unquestioningly. Coates wasn't just an author but the unofficial paterfamilias of the wokescenti. (Importantly, it wasn't Coates himself making this appeal but the cultural gatekeepers surrounding him. He won a National Book Award and a MacArthur "Genius Grant," among countless other prizes. Toni Morrison called him the intellectual successor to James Baldwin.) As such, I sometimes wondered if my white friends and colleagues who venerated Coates actually liked his work or just liked the idea of liking it.

From the black guys on Bloggingheads.tv, YouTube's algorithms bounced me along a path of similarly unapologetic thought criminals: Christina Hoff Sommers, a.k.a. "the Factual Feminist"; the comedian turned YouTube interviewer Dave Rubin; the anti-extremist Islamic radical activist Maajid Nawaz; and a cantankerous and then little-known Canadian psychology professor named Jordan Peterson, who railed against authoritarianism on both the left and the right but reserved special disdain for postmodernism, which he believed was eroding rational thought on campuses and elsewhere.

Some of them, like Sommers and Peterson, who I watched intermittently but in no way religiously, made their own videos. They turned these videos into their main platform and chief export, sometimes monetizing them via subscription platforms like Patreon. Others I tracked down in crude footage from university lectures or panel discussions with names like "Is Identity Politics Eating Itself?" Many also reliably showed up on *Real Time with Bill Maher* and, curiously, on the podcast of Joe Rogan, a comedian and mixed-martial-arts commentator whose guest roster of athletes, entertainers, and conspiracy theorists occasionally expanded to include people like astrophysicist Neil deGrasse Tyson.

Three years later, a handful of this cadre would be introduced to the greater public under the dubious banner of the "intellectual dark web." "Meet the Renegades of the Intellectual Dark Web" went a *New York Times* headline in May of 2018. (The article, fittingly, was by Bari Weiss, who'd written the opinion column defending Aziz Ansari in the wake of his #MeToo troubles.) The tagline continued, "An alliance of heretics is making an end run around the mainstream conversation. Should we be listening?" (Accompanying photos showed the subjects posing defiantly in settings like a rainstorm and a shadowy forest.) Within days, countless news outlets had picked up the story, and it seemed everyone had something to say about whether the members of this alliance had any credibility as either heretics or intellectuals. There was little, if any, consensus—descriptors ranged from renegades to grifters to white-nationalist trolls—but the fervor around the whole subject suggested a nerve had been touched, possibly even a major artery tapped.

For me, it was as if an obscure rock band I'd been following for years suddenly hit it big. I was excited but also a little worried. For starters, "intellectual dark web" was a terrible name. It reeked of sci-fi geek histrionics and, moreover, was too easily confused with that cybercrook-choked sub-basement of the internet known as the regular "dark web." Not that it was any better than the name I'd privately assigned them: Free Speech YouTube. *What will I do tonight? Make some popcorn and hang out with Free Speech YouTube!*

I didn't agree with my Free Speech YouTube friends on every point. Far from it. When Loury said he was skeptical of the claim that blacks got longer sentences than whites for the same crime, I scratched my head. When scholar and social critic Camille Paglia said that agreeing to accompany a man upstairs to a bedroom during a fraternity party is "consenting to sex," I cringed. But more often I was invigorated, even electrified, by their willingness to ask (if not ever totally answer) questions that had lately been deemed too messy to deal with in mainstream public discourse: *Are we using "multiculturalism" as a cover for tolerating human rights abuses in other countries? Can we use evolutionary psychology to help explain why women, in the aggregate, are less likely to pursue careers like engineering and computer coding? Are there biological brain sex differences that help explain the gender wage gap?*

You're not supposed to ask these sorts of things in public anymore. (Evolutionary psychology, which is all too easily oversimplified and repurposed into any number of shaky suppositions about social hierarchies, is a particular bugaboo.) Since my YouTube friends were asking nonetheless, many turned into de facto speech rights champions. And since the term "speech rights" now had a trip-wire effect for many liberals, in that it was often associated with defenses of hollow provocateurs like Milo Yiannopoulos, many of my YouTube friends were finding themselves cast out of the political left. (Yiannopoulos, by the way, was to me an imbecilic, insufferably boring varmint who bore no resemblance to anyone I found interesting on YouTube.) Not that getting cast out of the left meant not having an audience. Some of these folks, like Sommers and also Sam Harris, the neuroscientist, "new atheist," and host of a mega-popular podcast, were getting plenty of attention by asking these questions. Peterson, for his part, was poised to get very rich. I just got the sense that at least a few of them felt just as alone as I did. Their company with one another, even in the form of panels and webcam chats, managed to keep me company.

As I look back to 2015, I now see that my burgeoning relationship with Free Speech YouTube had to do with the end of another relationship, namely my marriage. I'd left my home in Los Angeles right after the December holidays and was living temporarily in New York. My husband and I were experimenting with what we had thus far managed to avoid calling a trial separation but was nonetheless a fairly obvious stepping-stone to divorce. I remember hunkering down in the small apartment I'd sublet for the semester while teaching at Columbia, anticipating a snowstorm billed as a "snowpocalypse" and watching something like six hours of conversations on Bloggingheads. For some reason the storm had me terrified. I'd been in California for so long that the thought of being blinded by a power outage caused by already blinding snow seemed beyond my coping abilities. But also for some reason—maybe because they were so much like the talks I had with my husband—the meandering dialogues had a soothing effect that evening. I lay on the couch and nipped at them all night as though they were brandy, finally drifting to sleep to the lullaby of conversations tagged "Should the left have a tea party?" and "Ferguson is not Palestine, but is it similar?"

The storm turned out to be not nearly as apocalyptic as advertised, and the power remained on. But in the ensuing months, whatever embers remained of my marriage managed to smolder out. I distracted myself by watching YouTube and reading everything I could about anti-rape activism on college campuses. It would be two years before I found myself at Iowa, sitting on the grass at Take Back the Night rallies and listening to stories like Joseph's, but I was already trying to sort out my feelings about the gulf between this generation and my own. I was all in favor of the new dialogue around issues of sexual consent, but why couldn't that dialogue be a little more, well, nuanced?

Many people I knew apparently saw it differently. They posted alarmist articles on Facebook and formed comment threads that were like a chorus of outrage and anxiety. When I saw them recite statistics I knew to be misleading—one in five, maybe even one in *four*, college women will be raped!—I wanted to scream. When I saw someone say she wondered if she should now even send her daughter to college, I wanted to throw things.

Even more than that, I wanted to put myself in a time machine. My crumbling marriage had made me something close to inconsolable, and my only wish was to go to sleep and fast-forward my life to some indeterminate point in the future when I'd feel better. By spring, my husband and I had decided to divorce. There was no tangible grievance, just a baseline dissatisfaction with our lives together that no amount of hard work or therapy or cable-drama binges could allay. We were in our forties. We had dogs but no children. There was no reason, other than the raw pain of finality, not to cut our losses and move on. I returned to Los Angeles after my semester in New York, and we continued to live together as we prepared to put our house on the market. We were amicable to an almost absurd degree, so much so that I decided I'd move back to New York, at least for a year or so, lest we remain emotionally entwined. Never at a loss for conversation, we continued to talk—often in the animated, passionate, probing way we'd been doing since our first date—until the minute I got in the car and drove east.

At the time, I assumed the extreme amicability of our divorce made us lucky. Whereas other couples fought bitterly, we just sat next to each other and cried. Whereas other couples changed locks on doors and let legal fees burn through their savings, we graciously divided up our things and did what we could to soften the other's landing. It was only later that I saw the ways in which this accord made things so much worse by ripping off the proverbial Band-Aid at an anguishing pace. It was only when we stopped talking so much that I realized how our conversations had been like platelets in my very bloodstream.

Despite our fundamental incompatibility, my husband and I were each other's best friend and preferred conversation partner. Even at our lowest points, even when scarcely a day passed in which we didn't fight, there was also not a day that we didn't have something interesting to discuss. From the very beginning, it had been clear that we saw the world in uncannily similar ways—and sometimes in ways different from our sprawling tribe of supposedly like-minded liberals. We shared an allergy to hyperbole, boredom with perfunctory expressions of political correctness, a guilty affinity for jokes best suited to adolescent boys. We may not have been on the same page when it came to life, but somehow we were on the same wavelength. We were, for lack of a better term, intellectual allies.

In the late summer of 2015, we sold the house, and I took one of the dogs, the hulking Saint Bernard, and moved to New York City. My plan was to be there temporarily, maybe a year or two, possibly three. Then I would return to L.A., where the dogs would be reunited and my husband and I, long divorced and healed, would function as both dear friends and built-in dog sitters for each other. The time machine would take off, orbit the Earth a few times, and land right on schedule.

But there was no time machine. I had to live my life in real time. And so 2015 drifted slowly into 2016. By then, Hillary Clinton, who was obviously and definitely going to be the next president of the United States, was talking about white Americans needing to recognize their privilege. Even when Clinton became the Democratic nominee, the residual heat of the Bernie Sanders campaign underscored the souring divide within the left. Clinton supporters chalked up any opposition to their candidate to misogyny. Sanders holdouts blasted Clinton as an establishment neoliberal with troubling ties to Wall Street. That there was truth to both sides hardly mattered, since cable news and social media lacked the capacity to metabolize more than two food groups at the same time. Meanwhile, the identity politics game that the left had been playing at a mostly amateur level for decades had officially been elevated to professional sport by the right. Its most valuable player, Donald Trump, would soon occupy the Oval Office. In the meantime, most of us on the left giddily prepared for Hillary Clinton to become the first woman president of the United States. We couldn't wait.

By that time, a year had passed since I left my marriage. My husband and I were still spending a fair amount of time on the phone together, texting photos of the dogs or running through our usual talking points about the thing we'd been chewing on since we'd met, a meld of politics, cultural observations, and personal gripes that could really only be described as *the problem with everything*. It wasn't the best of times, but neither was it the worst. The state of our marriage seemed hopeless, but the state of the world seemed at that point relatively intact. Until suddenly it wasn't. The night of the election, I sat on the sofa watching CNN and exchanging texts with my husband. The first text, from me to him, said something like "relax, it's still early." The last, hours later and from him to me, was one word: "wow."

I hardly need to describe what happened over the next year. Racists became more racist. Sexists hardened into full-blown misogynists. In turn, those fighting their bigotry too often commandeered their own kind of tyranny. Almost immediately, the resistance became not just a front line against

Trumpism but its own scorching battleground. There was no amount of outrage that couldn't be outdone, no wokeness woke enough. (At least not on social media, though, let's face it, social media had effectively become a placeholder for real life.) Amid this crisis, virtue signaling went from a kind of youthful fashion statement to the default mode of public and private expression. Twitter headlines wrapped themselves in the banner of social justice even if there was hardly a social justice angle at all. New crops of young journalists, many consigned to online opinion writing, knew all too well that career advancement depended on clicks, which in turn depended on fealty to the woke narrative.

From NPR to CNN to dinner parties in gentrified Brooklyn, you'd think the only conversations that were allowed were the ones in which facts were massaged to accommodate visceral feelings of liberal outrage. Sipping my rosé in the parlors of Cobble Hill brownstones, I'd hold my tongue as the permissible opinions ricocheted like bullets off the eleven-foot ceilings. *Of course evolutionary psychology is bullshit. Of course the conservative columnists in the* New York Times *are climate-change-denying troglodytes who bring nothing to the table whatsoever. David Brooks should fucking retire already! Amazing cheese, by the way—Zimbro?*

I'd say this happened every time I went out, but the truth is it happened about half the time. The other half, if people had enough to drink, they confessed the truth: they were getting sick of the term "gaslighting." They thought the pussy hats at the Women's March were a little silly. They didn't love

Ta-Nehisi Coates's book as much as they knew they should. Not that any of this stopped them from indicating the exact opposite on social media. There was simply too much at stake to do otherwise, they said. Apparently any admission of complexity was a threat to the cause. Nuance was a luxury we could no longer afford.

I still talked with my husband, but our conversations were growing shorter. Though the problem with everything remained an inexhaustible topic, the signal along which our wavelength traveled was growing weaker. In the spring of 2017, he called and told me he was in a new relationship and that we couldn't talk as much as we had been. It was a gut punch but also necessary and long overdue. I thought about calling a friend, but decided instead to console myself that evening by watching a two-hour interview on *The Rubin Report*.

The guest was Bret Weinstein, the biology professor who'd recently been embroiled in a bizarre racial controversy at the ultra-liberal Evergreen State College in Olympia, Washington. A few months earlier, in March of 2017, Weinstein had voiced opposition to an anti-racism event in which white students and staff were asked not to come to campus for a day (both groups, according to the college, would attend workshops exploring "issues of race, equity, allyship, inclusion, and privilege"). In response, student activists tarred Weinstein as a white supremacist and hounded him to the point that his safety was threatened. Weinstein and his wife, the evolutionary biologist Heather Heying, who also taught at Evergreen, would eventually leave the school and go on to become core members of the intellectual dark web. But at the time of the Rubin interview, he was just a guy who'd been thrust into the news following a traumatic professional ordeal and who seemed harried enough to forget that his glasses were hanging awkwardly around his neck during the entire two hours. He was also mesmerizing. He talked about intellectual "feebleness" in academia and in the media, about the demise of nuance, about still considering himself a progressive despite his feeling that the far left was no better at offering practical solutions to the world's problems than the far right. He talked about student activists who had accused him of white supremacy, who had hunted him down and threatened his safety. Amid the frenzy around his situation, he said, no mainstream news outlet except Fox had contacted him or covered the story. The concept of a left-leaning professor (Weinstein had been a Bernie Sanders supporter and was also involved in the Occupy movement) being accused of racism by even further-left-leaning students simply didn't fit the prevailing us-versus-them narrative.

"I honestly think journalists had no idea how to cover the story," he said.

I watched the video at my dining table while drinking half a bottle of wine. The next night I watched it again and finished the second half.

Let the record show: I was not completely without a life. I taught, at Iowa and also back in New York. I walked my dog.

I had dinner with friends. I stood at podiums and gave readings from my old books while trying to write—and rewrite and rewrite—the book you are now reading. But not having long conversations with my husband anymore had left a sort of white space in my life, as if there were a missing block of text in my line of vision at all times. Without quite realizing it, I crammed the space with the wonkish gladiator games of leftists fighting one another on YouTube. I watched symposium panels with names like "Are Young People Scared of Sex?" and "What's Wrong with Men's Rights?" I watched an American Enterprise Institute video of Sommers in conversation with Paglia, who recalled being a college student in the 1960s and fighting the administration over the unfairness of girls being subject to curfews when boys were not. "What we said was 'give us the freedom to risk rape! These are the freedoms we've won!'" I watched yet another video in which Paglia sat with an interviewer and expounded volcanically about the failure of the educational system and the collapse of Western civilization. "We're in a period of desiccated secularism," Paglia exhorted. "This migration, this transformation of the classroom situation and the university setting into a praxis to cure present problems. That is wrong! The university should be about abstract and detached study of the past and the global present!" She was totally bonkers and completely captivating.

I lapped it all up. I couldn't get enough. These videos felt like a safety net, even a warm embrace. Eventually, Bret Weinstein's brother, the mathematician and economist Eric

Weinstein, entered the Free Speech YouTube ecosystem with, among other things, a physics-based theory suggesting that institutional gatekeepers like mainstream media, universities, and even large corporations discourage complex viewpoints by labeling the holders of those viewpoints as bigots, idiots, or both. (Eric Weinstein, alas, was the one who would go on to coin the "intellectual dark web" label.) When the brothers sat down together for a two-hour-and-forty-seven-minute interview on *The Rubin Report*, I watched the segment three times over the course of a week.

And why not? Free Speech YouTube was what I did now instead of watching television (and, very often, reading books, listening to music, or cleaning my apartment). When a new Loury and McWhorter Bloggingheads video went up, my excitement was such that you'd think it was 1980s New Jersey and there was a new Springsteen album out. At a Columbia University event featuring McWhorter called "Identity Politics on the Right and Left" (for which I'd seen a Facebook posting hours earlier and hightailed myself to campus like a student late for an exam), I lingered afterward and fawned over McWhorter as though he were the Boss himself.

A simplistic reading of this story might suggest I had been red-pilled. That term, which came from the movie *The Matrix*, originally referred to being awakened into some vaguely defined realm of politically incorrect "truth," though it's now associated with indoctrination into the alt right and any number of related and troubling subgroups. But I found the red-pill concept facile at best, and not just because the conspiratorial overtones weren't my style. It wasn't just "truth" I was after. It was that pesky *nuance* thing. I would have taken equal, if not more, delight in criticizing the political right if there was anything remotely interesting or surprising about doing so. But bashing the right, especially in the age of Trumpism, was easy and boring, the conversational equivalent of banging out "Chopsticks" on the piano. Inspecting your own house for hypocrisy was a far meatier assignment. As with James Baldwin's line "I love America more than any other country in the world, and, exactly for this reason, I insist on the right to criticize her perpetually," I felt an obligation to hold the left to account because, for all my frustrations with it, I was still *of* it.

So this was no red pill that I'd swallowed. It was more like an assortment of pills of varying colors and sizes. When combined properly, these pills produced the desired effect of making me feel less crazy. If Heying, a biologist, a liberal, and presumably a feminist, believed that the best way to address the gender wage gap is to admit that there are biological differences between male and female brains that can influence women's professional decisions—"We can't make things better without first establishing what's true," she has said—then I was okay for thinking that, too. If John McWhorter said that Ta-Nehisi Coates's fans are engaged in a sort of ritual self-flagellation that's ultimately its own form of racism, then I wasn't a bad person for harboring the same thoughts myself.

Best of all, Free Speech YouTube wasted less time with

the "to be sure" disclaimers that now clogged just about any expression of not-perfectly-woke opinion. "*To be sure*, sexual assault is a terrible crime . . ."; "*Of course*, as a white person I can't understand the experience of any person of color . . ." Whereas newspaper op-eds and magazine think pieces seemed to devote three-quarters of their word counts to anticipatory self-inoculations from criticism, Free Speech YouTube generally dispensed with these catechisms. People just said what they had to say. They roamed fearlessly among my favorite subject: the problem with everything.

Just as often, though, the assortment of pills would make me slightly queasy. For every Free Speech YouTuber who had me cheering at my computer screen, there was another who I wished would just go away. The conservative journalist Ben Shapiro, for instance, struck me as little more than a run-of-the-mill right-winger who just happened to be willing to have respectful dialogues with his ideological opponents. Why exactly was he in the club? There was the problem, too, of Jordan Peterson's growing presence. Riding the wave of a public controversy over a piece of Canadian legislation related to transgender rights, Peterson had come into public view primarily as an abrasive critic of identity politics. That won him fans among alt-right types and other critics of political correctness and landed him in lots of montage videos in which he is billed as "owning" or "destroying" feminists or social justice warriors. His more thoughtful sides, though, earned him a place among the Free Speech YouTubers, some of whom became obsessed with him and talked about him constantly. In turn, my obsession with and constant talk about the Free Speech YouTubers put me in the position of defending Peterson—if not his ideas (many of which seem perfectly reasonable once you get past his bluster), then at least his right to exist. Not that I had any idea what either he or I was talking about half the time.

Within the year, Peterson's hybrid persona of philosopher king/anti-PC edgelord would make him about as famous as it's possible to be while still being a cult hero. By the spring of 2018 he was selling out large venues on international tours and netting $80,000 a month on Patreon. His best-selling book, *12 Rules for Life: An Antidote to Chaos*, functioned as a sort of New and Improved Testament for the purpose-lacking young person (often but not always male) for whom tough love directives like "Clean up your room!" went down a lot easier when dispensed with a Jungian, evo-psych panache.

But what was Peterson, exactly? A self-help guru? A men's rights champion? A grandstanding transphobe? Was he deserving of David Brooks's characterization as "the most influential public intellectual in the Western world right now"? (More precisely, Brooks had quoted economist Tyler Cowan saying this about Peterson.) Or was he, as one headline put it, "the stupid man's smart person"?

He's all of these things and none of these things, I said. *People are paying attention to the wrong parts of him. Not that he isn't calling attention to the wrong parts of himself. I don't know! Stop asking me! But keep asking me! Don't ask the people who understand him even less than I do!*

I was going a little crazy. My opinions about the different members of Free Speech YouTube ran the gamut. But they still felt like an obscure rock band I'd known about before anyone else and, as such, I was a superfan. And as often happens to superfans, I became not just the band's follower but its protector. *It's not* this *album that matters, it's* that *one. Forget the hit single and listen to this. No, it's not reggae, it's ska! There's a difference!* By the summer of 2017 I had managed to delete most other conversational topics from my brain in order to clear space for Free Speech YouTube. I did not care about the *Wonder Woman* movie or the solar eclipse or Cardi B. I cared about *The Rubin Report* interview with Bret and Eric Weinstein. I sent the video link to anyone I thought might be remotely interested (this included my ex-husband, though he was only marginally interested) along with detailed viewing instructions: *I know this is two hours and forty-seven minutes but it flies by, I swear. Skip the first three minutes. Pay extra close attention around the 1:28:23 mark when Eric says that it's possible we can squeeze another three hundred years out of this world "by repeatedly getting lucky" but that he thinks we're unlikely to make it that far. So intense!*

One spring night in 2018, on the cusp of a late-season snowstorm, I went to a real-life meeting for people who were interested in Free Speech YouTube. The gathering had grown out of *Quillette*, an online magazine that billed itself as "a platform for free thought" and that I had probably discovered within minutes of its launch in 2015. I looked forward to the meeting for weeks, hoping I didn't run into a scheduling conflict, even vaguely planning what I would wear. The

RSVP list suggested there would be a disproportionate number of very young men in attendance, many of them Jordan Peterson acolytes exhibiting rather alarming levels of worship. But that didn't bother me. I wanted to connect and learn. I wanted, as I said when I introduced myself, "to really dig into things" with people who cared about this stuff as much as I did.

It turned out that I had dug further than just about anyone. There were at least a couple dozen people at the meeting, most of them exhibiting high levels of Free Speech YouTube literacy. But for all their familiarity with the guests on *The Rubin Report* and Harris's podcast, I suspected my mastery had them beat tenfold. Their knowledge may have been thorough, but mine was granular. For every name they cited as "someone whose ideas really interest me," I could have hit back with ten more. For every Free Speech YouTube channel invoked, I could rattle off several no one had ever heard of. Eventually I got the feeling that I was talking too much, so I headed home.

The sky was heavy with waiting snow that night. I left the meeting and walked up lower Fifth Avenue in the darkness. There were few people on the street save a handful of last-minute shoppers gathering rations before the storm. School had already been canceled for the next day, street cleaning suspended, offices closed. It had been, I realized, more than three years since I'd hunkered down for the snowpocalypse in that little apartment, watching Bloggingheads and grieving over my soon-to-be-decided-on divorce. Amid this thought came a terrible realization: over these years, I'd weaned myself off the long conversation of my marriage by switching over to the conversations of Free Speech YouTube. It wasn't just political loneliness I'd felt; it was the loneliness of a partnership ended, a dialogue converted to an interior monologue. Having lost my human intellectual ally, I'd tried to rig up a new ally—or a whole group of allies—via internet videos.

I also wondered this: maybe my bloodlust for left-on-left warfare wasn't just a petty indulgence but a substitute for the warfare of my marriage itself. My husband had been at once the best thing about my life and the worst thing. He kept me sane yet drove me crazy. I wasn't so far gone as to draw a literal comparison between my marriage and my relationship with Free Speech YouTube, but there were ways that they were mirrors of one another. My Free Speech YouTube friends functioned as intellectual allies, yet they disappointed me as often as they bolstered me. Much as I was energized by some of the quieter voices in the movement, like McWhorter, Heying, and even science historian Alice Dreger, who left academia over censorship issues and had been embraced by intellectual-dark-web types even as she eschewed membership, I was growing weary of the self-conscious clubbiness of the whole thing. It was as if some of them were having the experience of high school geeks who'd suddenly been let into the popular club. They couldn't quite believe their luck, so they got matching T-shirts and wore them every day.

"It seems kind of, um, contradictory to consider us as a group, since the point is we are all bad at groupthink," Dreger wrote on her blog by way of explaining why she chose not to participate in the *Times* article. "If the idea is that I piss people off by being disloyal to my likely tribes, well, I don't think that makes me unusual. I think it just makes me a good intellectual."

A good intellectual, maybe. But being a public intellectual—or what passes for such a thing today—now demands sticking with viewpoints that can be represented by hashtags and squeezed snugly into nine-hundred-word op-eds or hot takes. It almost made me wonder if there was merit in becoming a public anti-intellectual.

"You're really on the right side of things."

Twenty-five years later, I can still see that man at the writers conference with the floppy silver hair. I can still see the woman with the jangling silver bracelets and the agent eagerly handing me a business card. (So much flopping and jangling! So much silver!) It was all so easy. It was a little intoxicating. It was also a lie.

If there's anything I've learned in twenty-five years, it's that the more honest you are about what you think, the more you have to sit in solitude with your own thoughts. If there's anything I've learned in the last four years, it's that being in a club doesn't guarantee satisfaction any more than being in a marriage does. Just as you can't fight Trumpism with tribalism, you can't fight tribalism with a tribe. All you can do is read and think and listen. And if you're lucky, eventually there will come that rousing, fleeting moment when you hear someone say the thing that makes you feel less alone.

CHAPTER 7

We're Not Joking: Humor, in Memoriam

I was alone on election night of 2016. I watched the tragedy unfold while sitting on my sofa with my Saint Bernard. Other than the handful of text messages I exchanged with my not-yet-ex-husband, I didn't communicate with anyone that night. And absolutely that night was a tragedy. Even in my allergy to hyperbole, I have no problem putting it that way. I went to bed before the election was called, hoping that somehow the situation would have sorted itself out while I slept. The next day, I got on the New York City subway and found myself in a car that was almost completely silent. Grim faces avoided eye contact; a few people were crying.

Less than twenty-four hours earlier, on November 8, I had ridden this same train and felt like I was at the biggest New Year's Eve party in history. People were smiling at one another, giving up their seats even for the not so elderly, practically twirling around the poles like children at a May Day fair. On November 9, it was like the bottom had dropped out of the entire city. I realize that's the kind of statement that makes a lot of people hate urban coastal types. I'm making it anyway.

For some reason on the night of November 9, I sat up late listening to Randy Newman's *Good Old Boys* album all the way through. The word "album" sounds strange to describe something you've clicked up on iTunes, but *Good Old Boys*, released in 1974, is a classic concept album, one of the most critically lauded of that era. The satire is so relentlessly dry it can leave your mouth feeling chalky at times. A blunt yet deceptively refined exegesis of southern bigotry, it's really about the hypocrisies of northern "tolerance." If you're familiar with Newman, it might be for his schmaltzy and sweeping film scores. He wrote the music for *Awakenings* and *The Natural* and a ton of Pixar films, including all the *Toy Story* movies. He wrote that awful song "I Love to See You Smile" from the movie *Parenthood*.

But these are Newman's day jobs. His real songwriting, which has a far smaller, if devoted, fan base, might be described as ragtime meets Tom Waits meets battery acid. His melodies can be hauntingly sweet, but his lyrics take no prisoners. In *Good Old Boys*, which was first performed by the Atlanta Symphony with Newman conducting (I mention this by way of conveying the ambition of the project), Newman speaks from the point of view of a number of Deep South characters of his creation. Those characters use the n-word and refer to white people as crackers.

The album opens with "Rednecks," told from the perspective of a slick yokel who opens the song with a defense of legendary segregationist Lester Maddox, the governor of Georgia in the late 1960s, who famously stormed off the stage of *The Dick Cavett Show* when Cavett referred to Maddox's voters as bigots. Tellingly, the narrator mistakes the effete yet fundamentally midwestern Cavett for a "smart-ass New York Jew." Maddox "may be a fool but he's our fool," says the narrator, who goes on to proudly describe his cronies who are "too dumb to make it in no northern town" and "keeping the [n-words] down."

Pointing out that "the northern [n-word] is a negro . . . who's got his dignity," the narrator admits that "down here we're too ignorant to realize that the north has set the [n-word] free." He then offers a laundry list of impoverished, crime-ridden neighborhoods in northern cities—Harlem in New York City, Hough in Cleveland, Roxbury in Boston, Fillmore in San Francisco—where this negro "is free to be put in a cage."

That's just the first track. There are also songs about the Great Mississippi River Flood of 1927 and the polarizing Louisiana Democratic governor Huey Long. In "A Wedding in Cherokee County," a bridegroom pays homage to his bride: "Her papa was a midget / Her mother was a whore / Her granddad was a newsboy 'til he was eighty-four." You get the idea.

When I sat up that night of November 9, 2016, listening to *Good Old Boys* through earbuds on my laptop, I was trying to build a wall around my brain. I was trying to have some sort

of immersive psychological experience, kind of like how in college I used to sit in the dark, the room glowing blue from the stereo lights, and smoke cigarettes while listening to Peter Gabriel and Laurie Anderson's "Excellent Birds" so I wouldn't have to think about my sociology exam or how lonely I was. I was trying to put a soundtrack to my life, thereby turning it all into a movie.

I'm still not sure what kind of movie I was attempting to place myself in that evening of November 9. I do remember feeling like I wanted to experience whatever I was experiencing as though it were in past tense. I wanted to have the sensation of looking at a screen image of myself sitting at that desk and knowing that what I was seeing was historical in some way. I wanted to take the time capsule into which I was already trying to stuff the emotional detritus of my failed marriage and throw in this film footage for good measure. I wanted to seal off the whole world and open it up again at a later, unspecified date.

I went to Iowa a few months later. I spent a week settling into the splendid 1900s American Foursquare house I was renting and the cold 1960s university building that contained my classrooms and office. Then I went about the arduous task faced by most professors, at least most writing professors: playing the part of a professor and hoping my students would buy my act.

My students, like all the best students, were equal parts invigorating and exasperating. They were dazzlingly well read but sometimes dismally clueless about how the world actu-

ally worked (which, let's face it, is a perfectly natural form of dismalness when you're a twenty-four-year-old). One day the term "gaslighting" came up. We heard it all the time. But what does it mean, exactly? we wondered in class.

"It's that thing men do to women," a young female student said.

Gaslighting is a reference to the 1944 film *Gaslight* (originally a 1938 play by British playwright Patrick Hamilton), in which Charles Boyer plays a sociopathic man who manipulates and plays tricks on his wife, played by Ingrid Bergman, to the point that she believes she is going insane. The term was commonly seen in psychotherapeutic contexts over the last several decades, but now the word was suddenly all over the place, a steady fixture in online conversations about how Republican lawmakers are hoodwinking the American people or how the mainstream media is normalizing the aberrant behavior of the Trump administration. It's also a staple of the feminist lexicon. To some women, the man who is offering up his point of view is automatically denying a woman her perspective—or "lived experience," as we now say—and therefore gaslighting her. Never mind that, in my lived experience, women's gaslighting skills generally far exceed those of most men.

I explained to my class about the film and the play it was adapted from. I did not admit that the only reason I had this information was that I'd googled "gaslighting" a few months earlier. I did not admit that up until then I'd thought gaslighting had to do with exacerbating an already volatile situation by adding to the controversy somehow. I thought of it as pouring gas on things and striking a match. My first encounter with the word had come on Twitter two years before, when I'd written a newspaper column about the tragic story of a transgender girl who'd killed herself by walking in front of a truck. An angry Twitter user accused me of "gaslighting the trans community." The sender of the tweet didn't elaborate from there, and in hindsight I wonder if the person didn't know what the word meant either, because for all the quibbles someone might have with what I wrote I couldn't see how any of it could be construed as making trans people feel like they were going insane.

But here we were. And as I gently suggested to my student that gaslighting wasn't something men did to women but rather an equal-opportunity form of bad relationship behavior, it occurred to me that I probably talked about this stuff way too much.

Why, exactly, did I care so much? Was I unconsciously perceiving my students' unrelenting wokeness as somehow an affront to me or my work? I had, after all, made a professional name for myself, such as it was, by testing the limits of propriety and skating on the edge of satire. Did I have some sort of personal stake in their abilities to develop a sense of humor and appreciation of irony? Or was I just taking advantage of the fact that my status as an as-far-off-the-tenure-track-as-is-humanly-possible visiting professor meant I couldn't be penalized, let alone fired, if anyone complained about me? Milling around the copy machines in the English Department office one day, I'd asked a professor of twentieth-century American literature if he still taught *Lolita*. "It's just not worth the risk," he told me. So maybe on some level I felt duty bound to give them what other instructors could not.

My rented house was about a mile from campus. I walked there most days, even the twenty-degree days that made time feel like a slow march across a frozen plain. On these walks, I asked myself over and over again why I was so determined to make my students uncomfortable. One of my courses was on the topic of cultural criticism. My syllabus emphasized intellectual risk-taking, controversial opinion, and even ribald humor. I wanted my students to understand that there was little point in going to the trouble of writing anything (and to write anything well you usually have to go to a lot of trouble) if you're not going to challenge your reader. I wanted them to understand that playing it safe defeated the whole purpose. But what exactly constituted "challenge"? Why did I assume that edgy satire was more challenging—not to mention more artistically significant—than earnest invectives against patriarchy and white privilege?

There was a part of me that wanted to force my students to sit down and listen to Randy Newman's *Good Old Boys* all the way through. Since there was no way I could make a pedagogical case for such a lesson, I settled for other forms of exposure therapy. I made them read one of my favorite guilty pleasures, Christopher Hitchens's 2007 *Vanity Fair* article "Why Women Aren't Funny."

I went through a spiel about how Hitchens was really making a feminist point (or at least what I considered to sort of be one) because he was essentially saying that comedy was a low art and women were *above* it. Then I forced them to watch the video Hitchens had made defending himself from the inevitable backlash. In the video, Hitchens maintains a self-satisfied smile as he blithely opines about female comedians tending to be either "dykes or Jews or butch."

What a cruel teacher I was! I was effectively prying their eyes open and forcing them to watch aversion therapies à la the Ludovico Technique in *A Clockwork Orange*! Watching their shocked faces, I recalled being made in college to sit through the Pier Paolo Pasolini film *Salò*, a grotesque interpretation of the Marquis de Sade's already grotesque novel *The 120 Days of Sodom*. The film depicted forms of torture ranging from rape to forced eating of human feces, and I'll never forget sitting in that dark screening room with my Vassar classmates from Italian Film Studies, gagging together even as we struggled to take notes in the dark. As I remember it, the collective gagging caused us to laugh, and from this combination arose a solidarity that rendered the whole experience too absurd to be traumatic, at least as far as I was concerned.

Nearly three decades later, I wondered what was keeping my own students from laughing their way out of discomfort. (I knew they could laugh at other things; I'd heard their chortles echoing through the hallways of the cold 1960s building that housed us.) Hitchens was a son of a bitch, but he was pretty damn funny and singularly insightful. Why couldn't they see that it was possible to be more than one thing at the same time? Was this not the essence of the intersectional theory they so adored? Or was I getting this all terribly wrong?

I taught my students "Isn't It Romantic?," the glorious essay by the brilliant, late David Rakoff, about the vapid sentimentality of the rock opera *Rent*. For context, I showed a video clip from the original Broadway production of *Rent*. The show hasn't exactly held up well. Based on the Puccini opera *La Bohème*, which is set in nineteenth-century Paris, *Rent* substitutes AIDS for the tuberculosis epidemic and essentially hands every character a death sentence. By the end, just about every character is infected.

Then, because I could not resist, I showed a clip from *Team America: World Police*, the 2004 raunch movie with a cast made up entirely of marionettes. Coincidentally enough, the movie, whose creative team includes the guys behind *South Park*, contains a scene (later cut from the DVD edition but easily accessible on YouTube) wherein the marionettes engage in coprophiliac sex not unlike what goes on in *Salò*. I did not show that scene to my students. What I did show them was a scene that sends up *Rent*. As far as I'm concerned, it is one of the funniest things in recorded history.

The scene is a musical number and therefore nearly impossible to describe in writing, but suffice it to say it features a character named Gary who's about to be recruited into a paramilitary anti-terrorism brigade. For the moment, though, Gary is an actor performing in the stage production of a show called *Lease*. We see him leading the grand finale, a song called "Everyone Has AIDS." Here he exuberantly calls out all the friends, family members, and pets that have died of AIDS. His delivery is akin to a preacher praising the Lord for his salvation.

My father (AIDS!)
My sister (AIDS!)
My uncle and my cousin and her best friend (AIDS!
AIDS! AIDS!)
The gays and the straights
And the whites and the spades
Everyone has AIDS!

It's a major production, a wall of sight and sound. It's a twisted hybrid of Christian rock, a Super Bowl halftime show, and Up with People, that slick but earnest traveling music and educational organization that you'd really only know about if you grew up in the 1970s or '80s. The song concludes with the word "AIDS" being sung for every note of a long, syncopated rhythm passage: AIDS AIDS AIDS AIDS AIDS AIDS AIDS AIDS AIDS AIDS AIDS AIDS: AIDS!

The singer raises his arm on the final note and then lowers it somberly. The audience rises to its feet in thunderous and awestruck applause.

I've probably watched this clip no fewer than thirty times. Never once have I done so without convulsing in laughter. The classroom in which I showed it had a giant screen. The video stretched wide across my students' line of vision, the puppets larger than our own bodies, the lyrics louder than our voices.

From my desk at the front, I was nearly falling out of my chair laughing. I was crossing my legs to avoid peeing in my pants. A few of my pupils were also laughing. A few of them looked like they might need to go to the emergency room.

The nice thing about teaching a class in cultural criticism is that you can basically shoehorn anything into the curriculum. Except Randy Newman's *Good Old Boys*, of course.

"So you see how the plague narrative has evolved over time," I said. "Puccini begat *Rent* begat *Team America: World Police*. I think that's enough for today!"

When I was the age of my students, HIV and AIDS were the wallpaper of the urban life. I was finishing up grad school in 1996, the year *Rent* debuted Off Broadway at the New York Theater Workshop. Though the official plague years were over, HIV awareness had gone from a public health initiative to a kind of fashion statement. Mandatory as it was to be a sexually liberated person in the world, it was even more mandatory to be terrified of sex and avoid it under all but the most risk-free circumstances. For a period lasting from the late 1980s until the first anti-retroviral treatments were approved in 1995, the standard prevention line was that everyone was equally vulnerable. It didn't matter if you were a gay IV drug user in Haiti or a corn-fed choirboy in Kansas. *AIDS doesn't discriminate*. I have a distinct, though now impossible-to-believe, memory of some kind of student health advocate at my college declaring during some kind of information session that there were "lesbians on this campus transmitting HIV to other lesbians." (Tellingly, there is a moment in *Rent* that hints at such a scenario.) In other words, it didn't matter if you and your partner got tested every other Thursday. It didn't matter if you had sex only with yourself. If you didn't use a condom every time, you were as good as dead.

Everyone knew this wasn't true and so continued to use condoms in the haphazard way people had been using them for years. But the disconnect created a cognitive dissonance that I believe left a mark on an entire generation. If college students and other young people today are obsessed with sexual consent, we were obsessed with sexual histories. I remember sitting across bar tables from men on dates in the 1990s and studying them for signs that they might once have had sex with another man or injected drugs. I remember getting tested for HIV repeatedly in my twenties even though I'd done exactly nothing to put myself at undue risk. I remember sitting in terror in the clinic waiting rooms because they weren't allowed to give you the results on the telephone. I remember becoming totally convinced in those moments that I was about to be called into a testing counselor's office and informed that my life was effectively over. I remember wondering how I would break this news to my parents, my friends, whatever sexual partners I'd had since the last time I was tested. I would entertain this series of thoughts even if I'd had zero partners since the last time I was tested.

Then the counselor would call me in and sit me down and open up a manila folder and tell me the test was negative. I would skip down the street in relief, at least until I passed the next "Silence = Death" public service ad at a bus stop. Then I'd freak out all over again.

Is this the reason AIDS AIDS AIDS AIDS AIDS AIDS AIDS AIDS AIDS AIDS AIDS AIDS: AIDS! is the funniest goddamn thing I've ever heard? Is this what leads to a world in which lowbrow, racially charged humor from singing puppets can have a forty-seven-year-old professor doubled over in stitches while her mostly early-twentysomething students either stare at her blankly or glower in contempt?

In my twenties and thirties I would try to explain to older people just how much of an imprint the AIDS crisis made on my generation, especially the sliver of us that happened to come of age right in that window of time when the disease had finally been recognized but was not yet under control. I would try to explain to baby boomers that the sexual revolution they had enjoyed was essentially in thrust reversal for us.

In recent years, I've had to explain the same thing to younger people. There is now medication available that lowers the chances of being infected with HIV by more than 90 percent. A gay man in his twenties once told me that he refuses to take this medication on political grounds because he feels it problematizes his homosexuality. Intellectually, I understood his logic, but nonetheless I found it stunning in its heedlessness. When I relayed the conversation to a friend in his sixties who's been HIV-positive for twenty-five years, he shook his head and said, "Fuck that guy."

The comedian Sarah Silverman, who is exactly my age, used to tell a lot of jokes about AIDS. In the mid-2000s she had a bit where she described getting an HIV test and being asked if she had a blood transfusion in the eighties. She mistakenly hears eighties as Haiti and says, "I used to live there." When asked how long she lived there, she says, "I don't remember, I was doing a lot of heroin at the time."

On the surface, it was a dumb joke. So was her joke "If we can put a man on the moon, we can put a man with AIDS on the moon. And then someday we can put everyone with AIDS on the moon." But there's something so Gen X about these jokes that I can't help but adore them. As with the humor of *South Park* creators Trey Parker and Matt Stone, who are each within a year of my age, the modus operandi seems to be to take the piss out of things. There must be something about being born in the late sixties through the seventies that triggered an allergy to earnestness. Silverman also had a penchant for Holocaust jokes (*What do Jews hate most about the Holocaust? The cost!*) and, moreover, rape jokes. Her 2005 comedy tour included this classic: *I was raped by a doctor, which, you know, is bittersweet for a Jewish girl.* In her 2013 stand-up special, *We Are Miracles*, she explained her logic thusly: "Rape, obviously, the most heinous crime imaginable. Rape *jokes* are great!"

But in 2017, when an interviewer for the *Guardian* quoted the raped-by-a-doctor joke back to her, Silverman reportedly looked panicked.

"There are jokes I made fifteen years ago that I absolutely

would not make today, because I am less ignorant than I was," Silverman told the reporter. "I know more now than I did. I change with more information."

That first part of that quote—*There are jokes I made fifteen years ago that I absolutely would not make today*—became the headline of the article. It's a good headline. When I saw it, I clicked on the story immediately. But the story didn't take me where I expected to go. I assumed Silverman was going to be lamenting the comedic drought in which we now find ourselves. I thought she'd echo comedians like Chris Rock and Jerry Seinfeld, who've publicly voiced their trepidation about performing for college audiences. "You can't even be offensive on your way to being inoffensive," Rock has said.

In a 2015 *Atlantic* article, Caitlin Flanagan (yes, *the* Caitlin Flanagan of the #MeToo mention several chapters back) described the scene at the National Association for Campus Activities annual conference, in which comics and others showcase their acts in the hopes of getting booked at colleges. As it turns out, colleges are the network television of comedy venues; only the mildest material makes it past the gatekeepers, though in this case the gatekeepers aren't General Mills or Procter & Gamble but students themselves. As a result, many of the most exciting acts don't get booked. Instead, performers deliver low-risk routines that, in a sad self-fulfilling prophecy, may reinforce students' preexisting belief that comedy, like so much else in the world, just isn't funny.

"These young people have decided that some subjects—among them rape and race—are so serious that they shouldn't be fodder for comics," Flanagan wrote. "They want a world that's less cruel; they want to play a game that isn't rigged in favor of the powerful."

Should societies be organized around their weakest members or their strongest? Should marginalized groups be afforded special status or integrated out of the margins and into the mainstream? Should trauma survivors expect the world to tread lightly around them until the end of their days? And since some trauma is invisible to the naked eye, does that mean every interaction should err on the side of inoffensiveness? If not, are we only allowed to punch up? And if so, does that mean those of us perceived to be on the highest rungs are left just waving our fists in the air, with nothing to punch?

Maybe. But I still feel like punching something a lot of the time.

CHAPTER 8

....

What's the Problem?

Until very recently, one of my most abiding ideas about myself was that I was young. The other was that I was tough. The former is ridiculous. The latter is just meaningless. Everyone loses their youth, and everyone is exactly as tough as they need to be at any given time. Another idea I had about myself was that I was a liberal and a feminist. I believe those things are still true, but I also now think those labels no longer serve me the way they once did. I actually think labels are part of what got us into this mess in the first place. Labels—be they badass or bigot, SJW or white supremacist—tamp down contradiction. They leave no room for cognitive dissonance. They deny us our basic human right to be conflicted. And as I like to tell my students, if you're not conflicted you're either lying or not very smart. (I also like to tell them, "No one will love you unless somebody hates you." I'm full of these gems.)

So what is the problem with everything?

Is it that we're all lonely? That we're needy? That social media has flattened us into one-dimensional objects, rendering us stupid, unsocialized, unhinged, ungenerous, unwell? Is the problem that the personal is masquerading as the political? Or is it that the political is taken way too personally? Is the problem that you can't trust anyone over forty? Or is it that you can no longer hear anyone over forty? Maybe it's that people over forty are slowly losing their hearing.

Whatever the root cause—and this is a tangle of roots, a giant fig tree siphoning our collective derangement from the crumbling earth—it's evident that this era routinely brings out the worst in most of us. Trumpism has made us feel that the world is out of control. In turn, we've forgotten how to control ourselves. We've become toddler versions of ourselves. We've given in to a culture in which narcissism is affirmed with clicks and likes on the internet and then *reaffirmed* in direct proportion to its alliance with in-group thinking. We're raising the next generations to fear its most original thoughts.

Sometimes I think the problem is that we're being let in on too much. We're not only getting front-row seats to everyone's dopiest inklings, we're getting backstage passes and discounted merchandise. Social media sneaks into our brains, steals half-formed thoughts, and broadcasts those thoughts before they're anything close to being ready for what used to be called "public consumption" (or, as we used to say, "ready for prime time"). I realize now that much of what I've been reacting to these last few years is nothing more than undeveloped versions of already undeveloped thoughts. I think about what this means for young people, especially teenagers, whose thoughts are *supposed* to be undeveloped, even stupid. I think about all the stupid thoughts I had as a teenager, all the uninformed, half-baked, insensitive, self-serving, grandiose, totally-embarrassing-in-retrospect things I said to my friends and my parents and my teachers. What if someone had handed me a microphone and invited me to say them to the whole world instead? Would I have taken them up on it? Of course. Would the world have been worse for it? Of course.

It's easier to define ourselves in opposition to something than in alignment with something. It's easier to browse clothing store racks, used car lots, and online dating sites and note what we don't want—no zippers! no sedans! no sapiosexuals!—than to home in on what we do. In 2017 a Pew Research poll found that nearly half of all people who identify as either Democrats or Republicans do so more because they oppose the values of the other party than embrace the values of their own.

Another study from that year, conducted by two political-science scholars with help from the polling firm YouGov, asked self-identified Democrats and Republicans how they perceived the demographic makeup of the other party. The results were astonishing. Republicans believed that 36 percent of Democrats were agnostic or atheist, 38 percent were lesbian, gay, or bisexual, and 44 percent were union members. The actual figures are 9 percent, 6 percent, and 11 percent, respectively. In turn, Democrats believed that 44 percent of Republicans were age 65 or older, 44 percent were evangelical, and 44 percent had annual incomes higher than $250,000. The actual figures are 21 percent, 34 percent, and 2 percent, respectively.

You might say these numbers are reflective of people's ignorance or incuriosity about the political process and the world around them. But what was most striking about this research is that the more respondents said they "closely followed the news," the more misinformed they were about the other side. This was not a poll of Twitter users. A poll of Twitter users, I'm convinced, would have shown that 100 percent of people believe that 100 percent of those who disagree with them are either evil or mentally ill.

Not to burst anyone's social-media-enabled bubble, but there probably aren't as many evil people out there as some like to insist there are. There might be a lot of assholes, but the number of *literal Nazis* that walk among us, as with the number of *men who hate women*, likely doesn't live up to the hype. But I am beginning to think the culture is effectively mentally ill, or at least notably unwell. I believe there's never been a civilization as emotionally needy as this one. I believe we've never spent more time lying to our friends on social media—*You look amazing! You're a genius! You're a goddess! You're a badass! You're brave!*—for the sole purpose of getting those friends to lie back to us. When we hear these lies, our egos can remain sufficiently doped up for a few more minutes.

I am convinced the culture is effectively being held hostage by its own hyperbole. So enthralled with our outrage at the extremes, we've forgotten that most of the world exists in the mostly unobjectionable middle. So seduced by the half-truths propagated by our own side, we have no interest in the half-truths roaming in distant pastures. So weary from trying to manage cognitive dissonance kicked up by our own gospel, we forget to have empathy for those grappling with the confusions of their own doctrines. We forget that, in the end, to be human is to be confused.

In the middle of writing this book, I went to my twenty-five-year college reunion. In full disclosure, I crashed the reunion, driving up there for the day, without a reservation, after a friend convinced me at the last minute that I should go. I'd never been to a college reunion. I have complicated feelings about college, most of them stemming from guilt over the fact that I often didn't bother to get to know people as well as I could have. Because I often felt like I was impersonating a college student, I had a hard time believing other people were actually for real—those protesters, for instance, the imitation radicals with their preposterous demands.

Seeing my classmates in middle age, though, I felt I did know them. I knew them because I recognized my weary face in their weary faces. I saw the ways in which the passing of time had yanked some of our certainty out from underneath us. I saw how life had grabbed us by the shoulders and shaken us ever so slightly loose from our foundational coolness. Not that we weren't still cool. We were just human now, too. We were human in that way you have to grow into. We were human in the way you can't be when you're twenty or even twenty-five. By which I mean we were in direct dialogue with our failures and limitations. Decades earlier, we'd been bright, shiny nothings. Now we were fully formed somethings in various states of disenchantment and disrepair.

At one point in the afternoon, in search of a bathroom, I turned a corner in a dark dormitory corridor and ran smack into an old friend. We hugged. How long had it been? Twenty years at least. She was in the middle of getting divorced. My divorce, as it happened, had recently been finalized. We hugged again.

Who would have thought it would be like this? How did this all come to pass?

How could we have expected to be any other way?

I heard iterations of these questions throughout the day. People were getting divorced, getting laid off, having child custody disputes, having money problems and health problems and dying-parent problems. People were despondent over Trump, but they were also following news coverage of the tides of student activism and thinking the waters were starting to lap a little too far over the shores. Back in the day, we had campaigned for South African divestment. Now the kids were calling for boycotts and divestment in Israel. We had been fierce advocates for gay rights. Hell, we were one of the gayest colleges in the country! (In our time, the most popular student social event of the year had been the Homo Hop, a rave party sponsored by the Gay-Straight Alliance.) Now gay was passé. Transgender activism had students turning in their professors over improper use of pronouns. Dormitory bathrooms were labeled gender neutral, which was fine! But we couldn't help but remember the unisex dormitory bathrooms from back in our day, when men and women thought nothing of showering in adjacent stalls. So why the big production? And, by the way, why so much racial discord? We knew it was time for a national "reckoning" with structural racism. We read Ta-Nehisi Coates. We supported Black Lives Matter, or at least said so on Facebook. But now, from what we were hearing, the entire Western canon of art, literature, and philosophy was being written off as white supremacy. How had this happened? What was wrong with these kids? Or was there something wrong with us?

It was like we could taste our irrelevance. It was the sour taste inside our very mouths.

It was a warm June day. The pansies and marigolds in the Shakespeare garden were in full bloom. The tulips lining the quad were holding on to the last breaths of spring. Wearing sandals and clutching bags of souvenirs from the bookstore, the alums strolled along the brick paths of the campus. In the time since we'd graduated, many walkways and buildings had been retrofitted to better accommodate people in wheelchairs. This had been one of the demands of the Coalition of Concerned Students during the Moynihan uprising in 1990. Other demands, such as hiring a rabbi, offering kosher meals, and establishing an intercultural center, had also been met long ago.

Those demands, at the time, had seemed so radical. Today they seemed so reasonable as to be a matter of course.

Oh, the irrelevance! The obsolescence! The creak of aging out before you even get old. The phantom of time haunted me as I drove back to the city in my seventeen-year-old Volvo. It followed me back to my apartment, where, for nostalgia's sake, I poured myself a glass of wine, typed "Peter Gabriel and Laurie Anderson" into YouTube, and listened to "Excellent Birds" with all the lights turned off. (The effect wasn't quite the same without the cigarette and the stereo lights.) I was in bed by ten.

In the ensuing year, the feeling of irrelevance became a near-constant companion. It clouded my vision like the membrane on the eye of a lizard, shielding me from what I couldn't comprehend, sparing me the mortification of my own cluelessness. It had me both staring at myself in mirrors and avoiding mirrors. It had me lying awake at night, contemplating the end of the world. Or maybe just the end of my world.

Woke me when it's over.

It's never over, though. Every day becomes yesterday before you know it, but there are always tomorrow's problems to look forward to. Tomorrow, the young people now nipping at my heels will be walking the brick paths at their own school reunions, feeling some combination of embarrassment and pride in how they used to be. The day after tomorrow, their kids might be colonizing Mars.

In the end, I think I've come to I realize that *the problem with everything* isn't meant to be solved. It's meant to feed us. It's meant to pump oxygen through our lungs. It's meant to give us something to talk about. It's meant to fuel comedy and inspire great art. It's meant to keep relationships alive until the last possible hour. It's meant to invite our smartest selves to join hands with our stupidest selves and see where the other leads us.

The problem with everything is meant to keep us believing, despite all evidence to the contrary, in the exquisite lie of our own relevance. What a gift. What a problem to have.

Acknowledgments

No book can be completed without the help of wise, generous, and patient friends and colleagues, but this one was the beneficiary of more wisdom, generosity, and patience than usual. My agent, Tina Bennett, has had my back for nearly twenty years now and I am indebted to her and to so many others at WME, including Anna DeRoy, Svetlana Katz, and Laura Filion. The extraordinary Aimée Bell at Gallery Books understood this project down to its core and had the courage and vision to bring it to fruition in just the right way. I am grateful to her and to the whole Gallery team, which includes Aimée's exceedingly intelligent and organized assistant, Max Meltzer, as well as the magnificent Jennifer Bergstrom, Jennifer Long, and Jennifer Robinson (they put the Jen in Gen X!). Benjamin Kalin provided meticulous and invaluable fact-checking and Jim Cholakis did beautiful copyediting work. I also thank Celeste Phillips for her sensitive and adroit legal guidance.

For their insightful and rigorous editorial guidance on any number of fronts (and whose assistance does not necessarily equal ideological agreement), I am grateful to Ruth Barrett, Kate Bolick, Aaron Gell, Vanessa Grigoriadis, Siobhan O'Connor, Alex Star, and Alan Zarembo. For their friendship, old and new, and for their willingness to have endless—and at times contentious—conversations about the topics covered in these pages, I thank Ingrid Abrash, Carina Chocano, Sara Eckel, John Franggos, Steve Friedman, Lisa Glatt, Cathi Hanauer, Heather Havrilesky, David Hernandez, Laura Kipnis, Tim Kreider, Dinah Lenney, Alison Manheim, Thorpe Moeckel, Anna Monardo, Sarah Wolf, Emily Yoffe, and all the students I both tortured and learned from over the years. Without their thoughts, my own would hardly be worth the trouble.

About the Author

Meghan Daum is the author of five books and writes a bi-weekly column about culture and politics for Medium. Her most recent book is *The Unspeakable: And Other Subjects of Discussion*, which won the 2015 PEN Center USA Award for creative nonfiction. Her other books include the essay collection *My Misspent Youth,* and she edited the *New York Times* bestseller *Selfish, Shallow, and Self-Absorbed: Sixteen Writers on the Decision Not to Have Kids.* From 2005 to 2016, Daum was an opinion columnist for the *Los Angeles Times.* She has contributed to numerous magazines, including the *New Yorker*, the *Atlantic*, the *New York Times Magazine*, and *Vogue.* A recipient of a 2015 Guggenheim Fellowship and a 2016 National Endowment for the Arts Fellowship, she is on the adjunct faculty in the MFA Writing Program at Columbia University School of the Arts.